Cross on a Hill

Cross on a Hill

*A Personal, Historical, and Biblical Search
for the True Meaning of a Controversial Symbol*

Slavko Hadžić and Joshua Irby

Foreword by Michael Green

RESOURCE *Publications* · Eugene, Oregon

CROSS ON A HILL
A Personal, Historical, and Biblical Search for the True Meaning of a Controversial
Symbol

Resource Publications
An Imprint of Wipf and Stock Publishers
199 W. 8th Ave., Suite 3
Eugene, OR 97401

www.wipfandstock.com

PAPERBACK ISBN: 978-1-5326-6356-7
HARDCOVER ISBN: 978-1-5326-6357-4
EBOOK ISBN: 978-1-5326-6358-1

Manufactured in the U.S.A.   10/30/18

Contents

Foreword

HE IS TALL, BROAD, dark, and strong. You would be wary of crossing him on a dark night. You would not be surprised to hear that he had been a boss in the Mafia, a soldier, a refugee, and a convinced atheist. But that could be your introduction to Slavko Hadžić, the gentle giant who is now a pastor in war-torn Sarajevo. He has been a friend of mine for several years: we tend to partner up in evangelistic missions in universities in UK and Europe. He is one of the most effective evangelists I know, a reaper in God's harvest. I have never heard him give an evangelistic address where people have not immediately been drawn to Christian commitment. Such is the author of this book.

Published in Bosnian in 2017, it has been speedily translated into English. He has written it in partnership with an American friend who has long lived in the Balkans, Josh Irby, and together they have produced one of the most fascinating approaches to the cross of Jesus Christ that I have ever read—and I have read scores. Drawing on the biblical proverb "A threefold cord is not quickly broken," they set before us and skillfully interweave three threads. One is the astounding story of Slavko himself. A second is an historical appraisal of what the cross can mean to different cultures and peoples. And the third strand is a closer look at what the Bible teaches about its variegated meanings.

The style is immensely attractive. It's the sort of book that grabs you: when you pick it up, it is hard to put it down. It is immensely accessible—a real page-turner for atheist, agnostic, Christian, or anyone else. It simply bristles with intriguing stories and scintillating illustrations but never deviates from the main purpose of trying to find out and explain what the cross of Jesus means. The very fact that it brings a Bosnian perspective makes it very fresh for the English reader, who will often be surprised by the learning in its pages—always offered with a light touch. There is nothing pious or churchy about the book. It is warm, honest, wide-ranging, and disarming, and it draws you into its story. I commend it very warmly and can hardly think of any type of reader who would not be hooked by it.

Rev. Dr. Michael Green, Wycliffe Hall, Oxford University

Acknowledgements

It has been a long journey from the initial idea for this book to its realization. We believe it was God who inspired the concept, who strengthened our hands for the work, and who guided our steps from the first thought to the final product you now hold. Above all, we thank God that this book has seen the light of day.

We also want to thank our families, without whom it would have been impossible to write this book. We are grateful for the love, understanding, and advice of our wives, Sanja and Taylor, and our children, Jovana, David, Israel, Elijah, Adeline and Zoe.

The eight chapters of this book that explore the Biblical perspective of the cross were adapted from eight sermons we preached, over the course of two months, in the Evangelical Church "Koševsko Brdo" in Sarajevo. We thank the members of the church for their feedback that allowed us to improve and transfer those sermons onto the pages of this book.

We also want to thank our dear friends who read the chapters of this book as they were forming and gave us helpful input. Among those are Mark Meynell, Karmelo and Ivon Kresonja, Michael Brent, Jelena Miličević, Jennifer Bliss, Ante Miliša, Matt Henning, and Rick and Katie James.

Finally, we are thankful that God has brought the two of us together. As Dr. Petar Kuzmić wrote in an endorsement for the Bosnian edition of this book, "it is rare that a Bosnian and American write a book together." It has been a journey of mutual encouragement and support, one lifting the other through discouragement and difficulty. God has given us the love, patience, and understanding required to bring this book to completion.

Even though only two names are on the cover of this book, we gratefully acknowledge the many others—family and friends, brothers and sisters—who contributed to this work. Thank you for helping make this moment possible.

Slavko Hadžić and Joshua Irby
Sarajevo, August 2018

Pronunciation Guide

THROUGHOUT THE BOOK, WHERE possible, we have maintained the local spelling of names and places. Since the Bosnian language is based on a phonetic alphabet, it is fairly easy to pronounce once the sounds are mastered. Here are a few of the special characters you will encounter in the following pages:

c as in the *ts* in *cats*

č as in the first *ch* in *church*

ć as in the second *ch* in *church*

dž as in the *j* in *joke*

đ similar to the *j* in *juice* but softer

j as in the *y* in *yellow*

lj similar to the *l* in *volume*

nj similar to the *ny* in *canyon*

š as in the *sh* in *ship*

ž as in the *s* in *measure*

Introduction

IT WAS A FOGGY winter day, February 2015, and we were on a hill outside of Sarajevo, the capital city of Bosnia and Herzegovina. For a moment, the clouds parted and we could see the city far below in the valley. It was in this city that we met—Slavko, a transplant from the southern region of the country, and Josh, a transplant from the southeast region of America. We were unlikely friends, from two countries, two cultures, and two languages. Yet, we were brought together by what some consider the most controversial and misunderstood symbol in the world—the cross.

That day we had escaped the busyness of the city to reflect and discuss the idea of writing a book together about the cross. As we stood on the hilltop looking down at the city, we could not ignore the challenges of such an endeavor. Two decades earlier, the same hill was used as a bunker from which soldiers lobbed grenades into the city below. In the 90s, Yugoslavia was pulled apart by nationalism and ethnic division. Battle lines were often drawn by religious distinctions—Serbian Orthodox versus Croatian Catholic versus Bosniak Muslim. Sarajevo, like many other cities, was caught in the middle. Over 100,000 people in the country died in a war that is still misunderstood and debated today. As we walked among the ruins of the bunker, we acknowledged that the cross was also a victim of the war. Its meaning has been distorted and maimed. We decided, for the sake of the cross that brought us together, we must write this book. But the question remained, can the true meaning of the cross be rescued from its misuse and misrepresentation throughout history?

Because of historical and personal experience, people have vastly different reactions to the cross. Some people fall to their knees in reverent worship, while others react with anger and repulsion. Some make crosses of gold and wear them around their necks, while others ban their use from the public arena in the name of tolerance. How do you approach a topic as complicated as the cross?

There is an ancient proverb that says, "A cord of three strands is not easily broken." To strengthen the discussion of the cross in this book, we have woven together three strands. In the first strand, Slavko tells his story of life upended by tragedy and war. In the second strand, Josh traces the historical evolution of the cross as a symbol from an instrument of death to a sign of identity. In the third strand, together we turn to the Bible in search of the true meaning of the cross. We hope these strands create a three-dimensional picture of this controversial symbol and illuminate the true meaning of the cross.

To guide you along these three paths, we have given each thread a unique symbol to help you distinguish whether you are reading story, history, or theology. As you weave in and out of time periods and tones, we hope you realize how the past influences the present and how the present influences the future. While Slavko's story follows the natural chronological order of a memoir, we have taken a different approach with the historical thread. Starting with today, we work backwards through time, uncovering the events that shape current perspectives on the cross. Finally, we examine these ideas related to the cross—the cross as a sign of victory, suffering, exclusivity, life, shame—through the lens of the Bible. We have provided footnotes for biblical references so it will be easier to read the relevant stories or passages in context. While we have worked hard to weave these strands together in a way that builds the argument, we understand that some readers may prefer to read one strand at a time. We leave it to your discretion and hope we have made it easier with the formatting.

In this book we write, unabashedly, from the vantage point of the Balkans. This is the region we both call home and the location that inspired us to write this book. Over the last two decades, large crosses have appeared on hills above cities in this area. Each time a new project is undertaken and a new cross planned, part of the community cheers while another part protests. If the true meaning of the cross can be unraveled in the Balkans, a place long associated with division and disagreement, then perhaps the cross can rise above the confusion clouding it. The issue of the cross is a global one. It is a symbol that cannot be avoided. And understanding the true meaning of the cross might just open the door to a new perspective on life.

That February day on a hill outside of Sarajevo when we decided to write this book we knew it required honesty and courage. We want to ask the same from you. When you turn this page, you will join a conversation about the most controversial symbol in history. While it is natural to avoid such difficult conversations, we often find the most meaningful discoveries arise from them. That is our hope for you.

1.

The Madness of Youth

"When a man stays overnight in Mostar, it is not the sound that wakes him up but the light. I know this from my own experience. The light welcomed me before I arrived, followed me during my stay from morning till evening, and later after I had departed it stayed with me as the main characteristic of my memory of Mostar . . ."

—IVO ANDRIĆ

IN THE SPRING OF 2000, I stood at the window of the apartment in Mostar I had inherited from my parents. I looked up at Hum, the hill rising above Mostar, and watched as workers erected an enormous cross. The Catholic church was building it to mark the 2000th anniversary of the birth of Christ. It would be large, 33 meters high (108 feet), symbolizing the 33 years of Jesus' life on the earth. Passions in the town were enflamed: Croat Catholics supported the construction of the cross but Bosniak Muslims in east Mostar signed a petition against its construction and Serb Orthodox, though nominally Christian, opposed the project, as well. The vice president of the Mostar city council, Milan Jovičić, a Serb, wrote to Bishop Perić and asked him not to place a cross on Hum.

As I watched the workers, I remembered looking up at Hum from the same window eight years earlier, during the spring of 1992, when the dark clouds of war hung over Mostar. War was encircling us (in Slovenia and Croatia) and closing in on us, but we had hoped it would bypass Bosnia and Herzegovina. The conflicts began in Slovenia in 1991 and lasted only a short time—ten days with several dozen victims on both sides—but then war seized Croatia, lasting much longer and resulting in many more casualties. We watched the reports on TV and hoped it wouldn't spill over into Bosnia and Herzegovina. This hope wasn't completely unfounded. Mostar was a modern, cosmopolitan city, one of three cities in the former Yugoslavia, including Sarajevo and Vukovar, with the most mixed marriages. Most of the city's people were against the war and ethnic division. It had been that way for as long as I could remember, and I had lived in Mostar since my birth, long before, in 1969.

I was born in May and received as the long-awaited son (my sister was seven years old) into an extended family with few male children. It was the time of Communism when equality among ethnic groups and the erasure of ethnic differences was encouraged. My parents were in a mixed marriage—my father was Serb and my mother Croatian. Our surname, Hadžić, is the second most-common in Bosnia and Herzegovina (the most common is Hodžić) and the majority of people with that surname are Bosniaks, although there are a few Serbs and Croats. My parents raised me in the spirit of "brotherhood and unity," and I, like most people I knew, never paid attention to ethnic differences. Through my childhood and teenage years, I always had friends from different backgrounds, and for some of them, I didn't even know their ethnic identity. I believe it was the same for most of the people in my community.

Not even my mandatory military service changed this. I served in the military in Split, in the Navy School for Reserve Officers. I always loved ships and the sea, so my time in the Navy wasn't difficult. First in the school, and then on the ship, we were from every republic of the former Yugoslavia. In military school, I had three best friends, the first was Daniel from Slovenia, the second was Frano from Montenegro, and the third was Milutin from Croatia. When I got transferred to a ship, my best friends were Igor from Macedonia and Abdulah from Zenica, BiH.[1] After returning from the Navy, I started to study at the College of Mechanical Engineering in the Aeronautics Department because, besides ships, I loved airplanes. My plan for life was simple: finish a good college, find a good job, have a good salary, find a good wife, have a comfortable life . . .

In my first year of study, I got an offer through my friend Oleg to work in a newly-opened casino. Because I had a plan for my life, I didn't seriously consider the offer, that is, until I heard about the salary. My first paycheck would be many times greater than what my mother received as the director

1. The abbreviation for Bosnia and Herzegovina.

of a hotel in town, where she worked at that time. It seemed I had found a shortcut to my dreams of a good and fulfilled life. I didn't have to study for years to find a high-paying job; it found me without a diploma.

Although, at first, I thought I could continue to study and work at the same time, soon after receiving my first paycheck, I dropped out of college. My new job didn't create in me any moral dilemma; I didn't consider gambling such a bad thing, and I didn't see any connection to criminal activity. After all, it wasn't drug dealing or human trafficking. No one forces people to gamble. They go willingly on their own to have a little fun, spend a little money, and sometimes they get some back. I thought the casino was like an amusement park for adults. How little I knew.

Through the few years I spent in the casino, I saw many lives and families destroyed. I remember a man who gambled away his savings, his apartment, and his car, who fought with his family, and, in the end, landed in jail because he started stealing at work to cover his gambling debts. There were a lot of stories like this. My first job in the casino was fixing and maintaining the gambling machines. But when my boss and the director of the casino noticed I was a hard worker they promoted me. From an ordinary repairman, I quickly moved to working in the office, and eventually became the "financial inspector." My job was to make sure the casino workers didn't steal from the owner. It wasn't long before I was the manager of three casinos in town.

With my promotions came pay raises, but instead of protecting the property of the owner, I took advantage of my position as "financial inspector" to take a cut of the stolen money from the workers in exchange for protection. The casino owner didn't live in Mostar. In addition to the several casinos he owned in town along the Neretva river, he had casinos throughout Europe, and even in north Africa. In an article entitled "Big Bet—Organized Crime Controls Gambling" the Center for Investigative Journalism of Serbia writes about him:

> "Serbia may seem like a real happy place for many criminals who want to engage in gambling, and the problems associated with this activity today have deep roots in the past almost till the very beginnings of this business in socialistic Yugoslavia. The first casinos started to open in the early 70s, and they were exclusively for tourists—only foreigners could use them. Also, only foreigners could open and run them. Žorž (Đorđe) Jablan, a French citizen originally from Cetinje (Montenegro) was the first to seriously start opening casinos in Yugoslavia. He managed dozens of casinos

scattered throughout the whole country, from the Croatian coast to the border with Greece.

The man in question was a casino owner of worldwide proportions: besides Yugoslavia, he had his casinos and gambling houses in a lot of European countries, most of them in former Czechoslovakia. With his business, he managed to even get to Africa—in Kinshasa, in the Congo where he ran a casino called *Playboy*. Jablan used the company Kin Stib, registered in Africa, to buy space in the luxurious Intercontinental Hotel in Belgrade at the end of the 80s. There he opened a casino that was then one of the most luxurious casinos in the country, so say those who gambled in that period. This casino operated until 1992 when Jablan suddenly closed it down and left the country. People who had the opportunity to meet Jablan personally say that he left the country because he came into conflict with Arkan, a criminal who was on the rise then."

Together with a colleague, I traveled to Belgrade to set up a gambling machine in the casino in Intercontinental Hotel that is mentioned in the above article. That was the first and only time I met Žorž, who invited my colleague and me to dinner to show his gratitude for a job done well and quickly. Žorž Jablan, in the summer of 1998, in a garage in the Hilton Hotel in Prague, was riddled with bullets from an automatic weapon and killed. Even today, the killers and contractors are unknown. In addition to working in the casino, together with the friend who introduced me to work there, we had a few of our own gambling machines in some cafes in Mostar. Young and healthy, I had a lot of money and a position that gave me a feeling of power. The bouncers at the casino were there to protect us in case of problems, but really there were no problems. If any arose, I solved them with money, connections, and force.

But on April 3, 1992, at 5:20 p.m. everything changed. The town shook with a terrible explosion. Someone—even today it is not known who—parked a cistern full of explosives and grenades next to the wall of Mostar's largest Yugoslavian National Army barracks (commonly called the North Camp among the people of Mostar), remotely detonated it, and caused an explosion. Chaos and panic ensued in the city. Telephone lines were overloaded with citizens attempting to contact their loved ones and were blocked for hours. There was no news on the radio, only hours of classical music. A cloud of smoke arose from the direction of the North Camp and into the evening you could see a line of vehicles with Mostar's citizens leaving their city. That night, the flash of bullets ripped through the sky above the city. I was confused and desperate. This war knocking on our door was a civil war, and I was a child from a mixed marriage—my father from one nationality and my mother from another.

A couple of months before that April, after the start of the war in Croatia, draft notices began arriving at my address. You knew when the postman brought a blue envelope that it was either a summons to court or a draft notice. Having graduated from the School of Reserve Officers, I left the military with the rank of Second Lieutenant Reserved. Answering the draft notice meant going to the battlefield to fight against one parent, half of my family—half of myself. I told my mother not to accept the notices and to sign nothing, but soon it wasn't the postman coming to the door, but a military courier. One day I opened the door to find a courier in uniform with a rifle and a draft notice. In response to the question, "Does Slavko Hadžić live here?" I answered, "Yes, but he is on a trip. I'm a neighbor that came by for coffee." Convinced, he left. But on April 3, everything changed. After that day, both warring sides were looking for me to pull me into the conflict. War was taking hold of our city, and it was harder and harder to escape the draft. I spent one final night in our apartment with my mother.

Right across from our building, across the Neretva River, was the military barracks that they were firing on from the hill behind us. Soldiers from the barracks fired back and tracer rounds flew just above our windows and over the roof of our building. The next day I went with my mother and my girlfriend of three years to my friend's apartment in another, more peaceful part of the city where there wasn't any shooting and no one would think to look for me. On TV, we watched the deadly furnace spread until the flames of war engulfed all of Bosnia and Herzegovina. It became clear to me that if I wanted to avoid being pulled into this war, one in which I would be forced to fight against friends, family, parents, and half of myself, I needed to leave. But I didn't know where to go, which way to turn, to the west toward Croatia or to the east toward Serbia. After a day or two, the shooting intensified and the shelling began. I called the casino where I worked but an unfamiliar voice informed me that the casino was closed and that the army had taken over the hotel where the casino was located. Hopelessness and desperation took hold of me. I didn't know what to do.

2.

The Spite Cross

"It is a political symbol of provocation and intolerance. In this way, it brings unrest and distrust among people in BiH, and it's rubbing salt into the un-healed war wounds of many people."

—HUSEIN KAVAZOVIC (2014)

IN THE EARLY HOURS of December 5, 2014, fog blanketed the city of Sarajevo, engulfing the surrounding mountains. From the ridge of Zlatište, where the city usually sparkles below, there was nothing but soupy white.

Out of the cloud emerged four young men who approached the edge of the road above the city. They set to work. From the ground rose a white post, not unlike a telephone pole, but one that had been hit by a car. It was damaged at the base and leaned lazily. The men wrapped a thick chain around the base of the pole and the other end to the back of one of their cars. Easing on the gas, the tires fought against the pavement and the force of the pole. At last it gave. With a crash, the pole fell to the ground.

Now lying prone against the hillside, the object was more visible. It was one 32 foot pole extending up from the ground, with another 13 foot pole attached horizontally to it about 10 feet from the top. It was a make-shift cross—a cross that now lay among the roadside weeds on a hill above Sarajevo.

Sarajevo lies supine against the slopes of Mt. Trebević, whose peaks watch over the residents below. An unimposing mountain, rising a little more than 5338 feet, its immediate proximity, rather than its size, have kept it a favorite of Sarajevans. In 1959 a lift opened connecting the city to the upper mountain. After perusing the shops of Baščaršija, the handmade products of coppersmiths, leather workers, and cobblers, one could zoom up on Trebević for a coffee and the fresh air far above the city.

During the 1984 Winter Olympics, Sarajevo shared the beauty of her surroundings with the world. Bobsledders raced along the ridge of Trebević on a track built for the occasion. While it could in no way compete with the steep slopes of Bjelašnica or the broad shoulders of Jahorina, Trebević offered an unparalleled view of Sarajevo and nature at the doorstep of the city.

But during the war in Sarajevo, the mountain's proximity and position had a darker application. It gave the Bosnian-Serb forces a clear shot at parliament and the governmental tower as well as the high rise residential buildings. During the four-year siege, many citizens lost hope of ever escaping the mountains surrounding the city. In all 11,541 citizens died in Sarajevo, many of them killed by bullets or grenades lobbed from the grassy hillside of Trebević. Since the war, two generals who led the troops on Trebević have been convicted by a war crimes tribunal and sentenced to prison.

Trebević not only provides a good vantage point down on the city but also a view from the city. On Sunday morning, September 21, 2014, the citizens of Sarajevo looked up at Trebević to see a white cross on the hill. The cross had been constructed under the cover of night, on the hillside of Zlatište, on the northwestern incline of Mt. Trebević, which overlooks the financial and governmental center. The reaction on the streets and in the media, was immediate. "The spite cross on the hillside of Zlatište is rubbing salt into wounds," wrote the *Avaz Daily*. "Insult from Zlatište," declared *Oslobođenje*, another local newspapers.

Fikret Grabovica, president of the Association for Parents of Children Killed in Sarajevo, said, "This is obviously one in a series of provocations, intended to realize their aim. That is to put a cross on Zlatište, the place where many citizens of Sarajevo were killed, including a large number of children. This provocation should not be tolerated."

The cross was built by the Association of Concentration Camp Survivors of Republika Srpska and erected on Saturday evening, September 20th, and Sunday morning, September 21st. Branislav Dukić, president of the organization, said the cross was made as a memorial for the 6,500 Serbs who died in Sarajevo during the war. He said, "We have raised the cross-memorial so it can be seen by God and can be seen and guarded by the Serbs."

But not all Serbians agreed with Dukić's actions. At a press conference immediately after the cross appeared, Bojo Gašanović, the major of East Sarajevo, called the improvised cross a shame for all Serbians. "This was done by someone who is not a Serb. If you are a man who wants to do this, then you have to comply with procedures and protocol. The Orthodox bishop needs to bless it, there are customs, it is not done this way, overnight."

Husein Kavazovic, Grand Mufti of Bosnia and Herzegovina, said, "It is a political symbol of provocation and intolerance. In this way, it brings unrest and distrust among people in BiH and rubs salt into the unhealed war wounds of many people."

Despite the reaction, as the sun set that Sunday evening, the spite cross still glowed from Mt. Trebević.

The cross was crudely constructed. The upright beam was concrete internally reinforced with steel bars. With its base cemented into the ground, it gently thinned until it peaked at 33 feet. Were it not for the additional cross beam, it would be just another electrical pole along the side of the road. The beam, a pressure-treated and painted tree trunk, was attached to the mast by two metal brackets. The cross was positioned on the north side of the road toward the city; its white paint visible from the heart of the city below.

Sunday evening, a group of twenty young men from Sarajevo ascended Trebević to visit the cross. They were on a pilgrimage of sorts. They traveled in the name of faith, but not in reverence of the cross. They came in anger. At their head was Mirza Hatić, a local hooligan with mafia connections who had already spent five of his 27 years in prison. But tonight, in his mind, he was defending the city of his birth, defending its honor.

"Imagine a woman, in my neighborhood," he later told a reporter. "Her three children and husband killed in the war. She looks up and what does she see? A cross. She has no husband, no little ones . . . I will die, but that cross won't stand. We aren't bothered by anyone, not even the Serbs, and we want peace. But those who try to alienate us won't succeed and that cross should not be here."

Tearing through the outer concrete of the cross was loud and difficult work. However, eventually the steel rebar was exposed and the gang reverberated with the excitement of a fighter nearing victory. But before they could deliver the death blow, police vans appeared from around the corner. The youths were handcuffed and left to sit on the street for two hours as the officers sorted out what to do. What do you do with people illegally cutting down an illegally erected cross?

By morning the young men were released without charges and Mirza was giving interviews to the media. "We did it for the mothers of Sarajevo and Srebrenica whose children were killed. We couldn't pull it down . . . If it's not gone in two days, we will go tear it down."

What is it about two beams, one vertical and one horizontal, that precipitates such a passionate reaction? Is the cross a political symbol of provocation and intolerance? Is it an insult to weeping mothers and heart-wounded survivors? What is this symbol that provokes both politicians and mafia and religious leaders and common citizens to respond so strongly? What is the true meaning of the cross?

The "spite" cross, although leaning from the attack of its first night, remained on Zlatište through the fall. It wasn't until a Friday morning in December that Mirza and a few friends made good on their promise to bring down the symbol on the hill.

"I said I would tear it down," Mirza told *Avaz* the following day. "The Police of the Republic of Srpska sometimes watch it, sometimes don't. We were waiting for them to leave and then my friend and I went and we tore it down. It was a little after midnight. I'm proud of what I did, and I'll do it again wherever they put it."

The internet was abuzz, many ready to crown Mirza king of Bosnia and Herzegovina and defender of Sarajevo. He was the criminal who took down the cross. However, more was destroyed during the fall of 2014 than two white poles connected by metal brackets. The very meaning of the cross was damaged.

According to Mirza, he did nothing more than destroy "an ordinary pole." But is the cross more than that? How did it become a symbol of spite? What was its original meaning? Only a journey back through history can shed light on this symbol that cuts so deeply into the hearts of all who look upon it.

3.

Beautiful or Ghastly?

"The most obscene symbol in human history is the Cross; yet in its ugliness it remains the most eloquent testimony to human dignity."

—R.C. SPROUL

A FATHER WAS ONCE traveling with his young son through Milan and decided to introduce his prodigy to the world of fine art. The father was excited because his favorite work, "The Last Supper," was at the convent of Santa Maria delle Grazie. As they made their way to the museum the father talked enthusiastically about the artist, Leonardo da Vinci, describing his history and technique. The son, who only came up to the father's chest, listened with interest. After arriving and waiting in line, the pair finally reached the room that held da Vinci's masterpiece. Unfortunately, a large tour group arrived at the same time and the father and son were swept up in the crowd and pushed to the front of the room, right below the nine-meter mural. The father stood, wide-eyed, taking in every brush stroke, wondering at the expressions of every character. After a few minutes passed, he looked down at his son and asked, "So what do you think?" The boy's voice came up from the din of the crowd, "I don't know Dad; all I see are some feet under a table."

In art, perspective matters. Some works are meant to be viewed up close, others reveal their true beauty from a distance. The cross, like a mural, demands perspective.

The discussion of the cross orbits around one central event in history. On Friday, April 3, A.D. 33, Roman soldiers crucified a Jewish man named

Jesus on a hill outside the walls of Jerusalem. For the Roman leaders, this was just another cross on a hill. However, two millennia later, this cross is still discussed and dissected, ridiculed and revered, criticized and commemorated. For some, it gives peace, hope, and love. For others it provokes disgust, fear, and anger. The cross of Jesus stands as a dividing line in human history. It also stands at the center of our journey to understand the true meaning of the cross.

As we will see in the following chapters, this one event, the crucifixion of Jesus, has multiplied into a variety of meanings. How can we sift through the multitude of ideas and judge between them? We need to gain perspective by seeing the cross in context. Jesus' death on the cross, while an historical event, is also a biblical event that fits into the storyline of the Bible. To look at the meaning of the cross, we must see where it fits into the meaning of the Bible. Many of the misuses of the cross develop by focusing on only one facet of the cross' meaning and then over-applying those ideas. This is tantamount to judging "The Last Supper" based on a view of Matthew's feet. When we back up, broaden our view, and take in the cross in its context, we can better appreciate its complexity and beauty.

There is an often-forgotten story in the last chapter of Luke's gospel that speaks to this issue of perspective. On the Sunday morning after Jesus' crucifixion, two men were walking from Jerusalem to their home seven miles away, discussing the events of the weekend. These men had been followers of Jesus; they had heard his teaching and witnessed his miracles. When the Passover weekend began, they had been full of hope that Jesus was the Messiah, the Christ, the one who would redeem Israel. Yet, on Friday they had seen him turned over to the Romans by the religious leaders and crucified. How could this "prophet mighty in deed and word before God" have suffered such a fate? Added to this confusion, some members of their company went to the tomb that morning and found it empty.

As they were discussing these events, Jesus came up alongside them on the road, although they did not recognize him. He asked the men what they were talking about. The men stopped in their tracks and turned sadly toward Jesus in disbelief. "Are you the only visitor to Jerusalem who does not know the things that have happened there in these days?"[1] After listening to their explanation of the events, Jesus said to them, "O foolish ones, and slow of heart to believe all that the prophets have spoken! Was it not necessary that the Christ should suffer these things and enter into his

1. Luke 24:18

11

glory?" Luke, the author, goes on to explain that "beginning with Moses and all the Prophets, [Jesus] interpreted to them in all the Scriptures the things concerning himself."[2] The men were so moved by Jesus' words that they urged him to stay and eat with them when they arrived home. At the dinner table, Jesus took the bread, blessed and broke it, and gave it to them. At that moment, their eyes were opened and they knew it was Jesus. Just as quickly as Jesus had come to them, he was gone. In their excitement, the men rushed back to Jerusalem that very hour to tell the disciples what had happened.

Before Jesus' appearance, these men knew about the cross. What they lacked was perspective. They were looking at the bottom of the mural saying, "I can't see the beauty in this." However, once the cross was put into the context of the whole story—from Moses to the Prophets to the Resurrection—these saddened, travel-weary men had the strength to walk/run/sprint the seven miles back to Jerusalem. The cross is not an isolated event. It is the central event of the biblical story. Like the two men on the road from Jerusalem, we will not understand the true meaning of the cross without seeing it in its context.

Buying a diamond engagement ring has become popular in many countries over the past half century. The scene is sometimes depicted in film. The nervous young man walks into a jewelry store to buy the perfect ring for his sweetheart. He looks lost and confused. The sales agent brings him over to the display case and takes out various cuts and settings, placing them on the counter. "Do any of these catch your fancy?" The young man picks up one of the rings and checks the price tag. His face goes white. The small clear rock costs more than anything he's bought before. Sweat begins to form on his forehead.

Unlike the character above, a wise young man does research before walking into a jewelry store. He knows the terminology and the right questions to ask. "How many carats is that diamond?" "Let me see something in a princess cut." He asks to see the diamond out of the setting. He looks at it through a magnifying glass, turns it around in the light, examines it from all angles. He checks the color of the diamond against a white sheet of paper. He verifies the weight for himself. A wise young man does these things because he wants to know the true value of the diamond before he buys it, because he wants his fiancée to glance down lovingly at the ring

2. Luke 24:25–27

long after they are married, and because he doesn't want to be cheated by an over eager salesman. In short, he examines the diamond closely because he wants to make the right choice.

The same is true with the cross. The cross is a complex symbol and to understand its true value you must turn it around in your hand, look at it from different angles, and observe each facet of it. Is the cross a symbol of exclusivity or inclusivity? Is it a symbol of death or life? Is it a symbol of victory or shame? By understanding each facet of the cross in the context of the Bible's story, we can draw near to its full meaning.

The historical fact that Jesus died on a cross on a hill outside of Jerusalem is undisputed within the academic world. New Testament scholar Dominic Crossan writes, "That he was crucified is as sure as anything historical can ever be." Even Reza Aslan, a Muslim academic who treats the New Testament as a man-made document, states clearly and conclusively in his recent book that "Jesus was crucified by Rome." The fact of the event is undeniable. However, the question of meaning remains. What does the cross mean as the central event of the biblical story? What does that mean for us today? In the following chapters, we will both step back and gain perspective and step forward and examine the cross closely through the lens of the Bible.

In the end, perspective matters. When Friedrich Nietzsche looked at the cross he saw something ghastly. He wrote, "The god on the cross is a curse on life and a sign to seek relief from it." Thomas à Kempis, in contrast, saw before him a mural of great beauty. "In the Cross is salvation; in the Cross is life; in the Cross is protection against our enemies; in the Cross is infusion of heavenly sweetness; in the Cross is strength of mind; in the Cross is joy of spirit; in the Cross is excellence of virtue; in the Cross is perfection of holiness. There is no salvation of soul, nor hope of eternal life, save in the Cross."

4.

The Thunder of War

"There has never been a good war, or a bad peace."
—BENJAMIN FRANKLIN

THE CITY HAD ALREADY seen several days of gunfire when the grenades started to fall. My girlfriend Sanja, my mother, and I went to a part of the town called Cernica where my father's elderly aunt, Staka, lived. Born at the turn of the century, she was then 92 years old. We went to see her because we were worried how she was getting along. We found her in her room watching TV—a travel show about Polynesia. Just the fact that a war was starting and the town was filled with gunfire and grenades, yet the TV station was showing a travel show about Polynesia encapsulates the thoughtlessness and absurdity of war. After making sure Staka was okay, we started back. I never saw her again. Some of the neighbors were standing on a street corner watching through binoculars as soldiers atop Hum launched mortar bombs. We started through town, skirting the edges of houses trying to find some shelter from the snipers and the grenades.

As we passed one of the traditional churches that had survived in the city during the time of Communism, Sanja asked if it would bother me if she went inside and prayed for us. It was a logical question because two and half years ago when I asked her to start dating, I gave her two conditions. Sanja came from a religious family—her parents went to church, baptized their children, and gave them religious education even during the time of communism. I was a declared and convinced atheist, whose parents taught there was no God, who learned in school there was no God, and who didn't

14

like religion or anything connected to it. I liked Sanja, but I didn't like her religiousness, so I asked her to stop going to church (which she still sometimes did, but not as often as when she was a child), and to take off her little cross earrings. Those crosses, though nice little golden decorations, offended my eyes and reminded me of something I was against, something I couldn't endorse.

After the fall of Communism, national religious tensions grew and intensified, and I blamed the poisoning of the political situation in the country, in part, on religion and religious symbols including the cross. Sanja liked me more than the religion and tradition of her family, so she agreed to my conditions, removed the earrings and stopped going to church. Or she did until that day in April 1992. I stood with her in front of the church building totally desperate and confused. I wasn't used to being in situations I couldn't control—I was young and strong, a boss of three casinos, I had money and friends. I didn't have any major problems in life, and if anything came up, I solved it with money, connections, or force.

And yet, there I was, standing with Sanja in front of the church, and for the first time I felt helpless and hopeless. No money, connections, or force could help me, and I didn't know what to do. I answered Sanja's question and she was shocked when I told her to go and pray and that I would wait outside. I watched as she entered through the big church doors; I stood outside and waited. Minutes passed, and she didn't return, so I entered through those large, heavy, wooden doors and into the darkness. The church was empty, and I saw Sanja on the right praying as I stood behind the door. On the wall across from me was a large cross, a symbol of offense to me, a symbol I had mocked my whole life. However, the sense of hopelessness and desperation was greater than my aversion to the cross, so I closed my eyes and silently prayed for the first time in my life.

I didn't know how to pray, so my first prayer was very short and simple: "God, if you exist, please help me and show me what to do." I thought that if God exists and if I ask him for something, then I probably need to give him something in return because in life I learned if someone does me a favor I have to return it. So, I listed some promises, things I would do and things he could ask of me if he answered my prayer.

I opened my eyes . . . and nothing spectacular happened . . . no angels, fanfare, or fireworks. I left a little disappointed and waited outside for Sanja. I didn't tell her I went into the church and prayed, but from that moment on something started to change. I started to feel an inner peace. The cross, which I believed contributed to the start of the war in my country, started to bring peace in my heart. A few days later, we decided to leave Mostar and Bosnia and Herzegovina.

The decision we made was a little strange. Sanja is Croatian (both her parents are Croatian), and I am a child of a mixed marriage (father-Serb, mother-Croatian). A few days earlier, Sanja's parents escaped to Makarska, Croatia. Sanja and I, together three-quarters Croatian, decided to go to Serbia. We went to my apartment, and at the entrance to my neighborhood we came upon a military barricade. One of the guys at the barricade was the boyfriend of Sanja's cousin, so we got through and returned without a problem. We were in the apartment only long enough to grab a few necessary items: money, documents, and some clothes. Then we went to Đikovina, to Sanja's house, to take some of her clothes and documents.

As we were leaving, we saw the silhouettes of Serbian soldiers on Hum, and from the basement of the house across the road Croatian soldiers started shouting at us, telling us to run away because a sniper was shooting from the hill. I was carrying Sanja's bag in one hand and her cat, that we were planning to leave with a friend, in the other. When the soldiers started to yell, I threw the cat and the bag in the back seat of the car, cranked on the engine, and took off towards town. The cat, scared to death, leapt onto my head. If we weren't at the start of a war and if the situation wasn't so tragic, it would have been more than funny.

That afternoon we said goodbye to our friends and started our journey. My mom and my little nephew and niece went with us. My sister and brother-in-law stayed in Mostar to try to protect their apartment from burglars, who were taking advantage of the chaos and anarchy, but they planned to join us later, if the situation got worse. We took only a few things with us because in our hearts we hoped this insanity would stop soon and we would return home quickly. I didn't have enough gas in the car, and the gas stations weren't working. I went to Oleg's father, Pero, who drew the last liters of gas from his car with a hose and gave it to me.

We headed out toward Bjelušine, by the Orthodox graveyard, because they announced on the radio that a sniper was shooting at cars in Donja Mahala, and there were casualties. At the edge of town we came upon a barricade of civilians with automatic rifles. I slowed down and put my hand on the handle of the pistol that was underneath the seat. As worry consumed me, I saw familiar faces. At the barricade were guys that I knew and who had often gambled in the casino. I stopped, greeted them, we exchanged a few sentences and they waved me on.

A half an hour after we left Mostar, as we were passing through Nevesinje, a drunk reservist near my car fired off a round from an AK-47 in the air, which really scared us. Upon entering Gacko my tire went flat, and since we had a long way ahead of us, I stopped at the first tire shop to patch it up. He charged ten times the normal amount—some people were already profiting from the war. Because we left Mostar late in the afternoon, we slept in east Herzegovina at the weekend house of my (future) best man Oleg and started again the next morning. At the Montenegrin border, there was a police patrol monitoring and recording all who passed through. My mom was afraid that as a young man fit for military service they wouldn't let me out of Bosnia and Herzegovina, however, the police just wrote down our information and let us pass.

Shortly after the checkpoint, we passed by a line of tanks heading toward Herzegovina. On the road toward Serbia, we met several other larger military divisions on the move. We arrived in Belgrade late in the afternoon where my father's family graciously received us and cared for us, but many problems still remained. First, in Serbia there was a mandatory draft, and if the police identified you on the street with BiH documents, they would detain you without discussion and send you to the battlefield. Secondly, the situation quickly intensified so that my brother-in-law couldn't leave Mostar, and my sister couldn't come to Serbia. Even though my father's family lived in a big house, they had only one bedroom, so the five of us slept on the floor in the living room. After a few days, we moved to the apartment of another relative who was living in Cyprus with her family and whose apartment was unoccupied.

Days passed by slowly, and every day we watched the news and spoke with acquaintances on the telephone to try to keep up with the latest information. Almost every day I went to Knez Mihailova Street in front of the Moskva Hotel where refugees from BiH gathered. Each day there were more and more refugees, and I started to see familiar faces, even some friends from Mostar. Because my nephew and niece were small (seven and eight years old), my mother decided to travel with them across Hungary to Makarska, Croatia, to meet up with my sister who had succeeded in getting out of Mostar. I thought that if my mother left and they drafted me, Sanja would be all alone in the midst of a conflict, a Croatian in Serbia without her friends or her family.

I didn't want to go back to the war, but I also didn't want to stay in Serbia because of the draft. A third option remained: to keep moving. The problem was adult males needed permission from the military to leave the country, which I had no chance of getting. Desperation again gripped my heart and I remembered praying just a few days before in Mostar a prayer that brought peace in the place of desperation, a prayer that preceded our escape from the war zone. Once again, I prayed.

5.

The Fiery Cross

"Look at our lights on the mountains! They are ablaze—

range on range our signals gleam until the Fiery Cross is lost among the stars!"

—THE CLANSMAN, THOMAS DIXON

THE MORNING OF APRIL 27, 1960, a black man in his early thirties descended the steps of his Atlanta home. He was dressed in a dark suit—his tie neatly knotted and shoes meticulously shined. Beside him walked a two-year-old boy, his son. The house was the one he grew up in, which he now rented from the Baptist church his father pastored. Four months earlier they had resettled in Atlanta after many years away. During that time, he graduated from seminary in Pennsylvania and earned a doctorate in theology in Boston. Like his father, he too was a Baptist minister. The previous five years he spent as the senior pastor of a Baptist church in Montgomery, Alabama. His return to Atlanta was to find enough rest and quiet to think and write.

The man, closely followed by his son, crossed into the yard from the front steps. Bending at the waist, he grasped a 5 foot stick haphazardly staked in the dirt. It was wrapped in burlap cloth, now blackened and charred, and it smelled of kerosene. The stick had a crossbeam so that it formed the shape of a cross—a cross that was ablaze the night before. Under the watchful eye of his son Marty, Dr. Martin Luther King, Jr. calmly pulled the cross from the earth in front of his house.

While history does not record who placed the flaming cross in King's yard that April, the message was clear: you, and your kind, don't belong here.

How did the cross become a symbol of hatred and division? Is this what the cross means?

The earliest historical reference to a flaming cross comes from the Scottish Highlands. In a time before electric light and modern communication, the fiery cross, or *Crann Tara*, was used by the mountain clans to rally their men to battle. A fiery cross on a hill could be seen from a great distance and alerted the clan to imminent danger.

The clans would also use another means of rallying men to battle. The chieftain would make a small cross of soft wood and light the four ends of it on fire. He would then extinguish the flames with the blood of a sacrificed goat. The cross was then carried from village to village where the bearer would speak only one word: the place for meeting. This tradition carried with it the understanding that any able-bodied man who refused to mobilize would meet the same fate as the goat and the cross.

The Crann Tara was immortalized in the epic poem *The Lady of the Lake* by Sir Walter Scott.

> "Yet live there still who can remember well,
> How, when a mountain chief his bugle blew,
> Both field and forest, dingle, cliff; and dell,
> And solitary heath, the signal knew;
> And fast the faithful clan around him drew.
> What time the warning note was keenly wound,
> What time aloft their kindred banner flew.
> While clamorous war-pipes yelled the gathering sound,
> And while the Fiery Cross glanced, like a meteor, round."

While the ceremony of Crann Tara was surrounded by the elements of religion, it is clear, even in the poetry of Sir Walter Scott, that the flaming cross "had more of blasphemy than prayer."

> "The shout was hushed on lake and fell,
> The Monk resumed his muttered spell.
> Dismal and low its accents came,
> The while he scathed the Cross with flame;
> And the few words that reached the air,

Although the holiest name was there,
Had more of blasphemy than prayer.
But when he shook above the crowd
Its kindled points, he spoke aloud:—
'Woe to the wretch who fails to rear
At this dread sign the ready spear!
For, as the flames this symbol sear,
His home, the refuge of his fear,
A kindred fate shall know.'"

The fiery cross was a means of communication for the Scottish clans. And what did it communicate? Rally to the defense of your brothers or face a shameful fate. But how did the fiery cross make its way across the ocean and to a front yard in Atlanta?

After the American Civil War, many white southerners felt threatened by the changes imposed by Reconstruction (the conditions set by the federal government that would allow the southern states back into the Union). They feared the influx of northerners (derogatorily called "carpetbaggers") moving to the south and the integration of newly-freed black men and women. At the end of 1865 and the beginning of 1866, some of these southern war veterans began to resist these changes with insurgent violence. They went by many names but the one that emerged over the following years was the Ku Klux Klan. Over the course of the next five years, members of the KKK killed tens of thousands of black freedmen and their white supporters, staged political riots, and spread terror throughout the south. They preferred to ride at night and wore robes and masks to hide their identity. Their goal was to create fear and preserve a past that was slipping away.

In the end, the first Klan was short-lived. The U.S. Government took steps to outlaw and disband these insurgent groups. However, the seeds of discontent were planted and would later bloom into their full terror.

In 1905, a playwright and Baptist minister who grew up in North Carolina during the post-civil war reconstruction, penned a novel that would lead to the re-emergence of the KKK. Angered by the representation of southern whites in Harriet Beecher Stowe's *Uncle Tom's Cabin*, Thomas Dixon wrote a "Trilogy of Reconstruction" that, among other things, romanticized the role of the KKK in protecting the southern way of life. The middle book, *The Clansman*, had the deepest affect.

In the most chilling scene of the novel, which was made into the movie *Birth of a Nation* (1915), a freed slave, Gus, now a military captain under Reconstruction, announces his intentions to marry the little sister of a white Confederate colonel. When she refuses, he chases her into the woods. At last, he corners her at the edge of a cliff. The girl, realizing she is trapped, throws herself from the cliff and to her death. When her brother finds her, he gathers a small group of clansmen to seek justice. They make a small cross of only 8 inches, drench it in the girl's blood, and set it on fire. Then, after capturing the black captain, they hold an unofficial trial and execute him by hanging.

An illustration accompanies this scene in the book. In the background, there is a ring of white-cloaked figures watching in approval. In the foreground, an elderly man with white hair and beard holds a small cup, presumably with the blood of the slain girl, while a younger man holds aloft a small cross with flames leaping from its three points. At their feet, in the dark, is Gus, bound and awaiting his fate. The title below the drawing says, "The Fiery Cross of old Scotland's hills!"

On November 25, 1915, an itinerant Methodist preacher, William Joseph Simmons, took fifteen friends to the top of Stone Mountain outside of Atlanta. The summit of the rock dome stands 820 feet above the surrounding land and was chosen by Simmons for its visibility. Inspired by the images in *Birth of a Nation* and drawn to Scottish traditions during the "racially purer times" of medieval Europe, Simmons ascended Stone Mountain to rebirth the Ku Klux Klan. The men, clad in white hoods and cloaks, encircled a makeshift altar on which lay an American flag, a Bible, and an unsheathed sword. As Simmons muttered incantations, they were bathed in the orange glow of a 16 foot tall burning cross. Simmons recounts the occasion:

> "Bathed in the sacred glow of the fiery cross, the Invisible Empire was called from its slumber of half-a-century to take up a new task and fulfill a new mission for humanity's good and to call back to mortal habitation the good angel of practical fraternity among men."

Within ten years, the Ku Klux Klan claimed four million members in America—marching in parades, wearing hoods, and lighting crosses. Fueled by a radical patriotism, compelled by a fear of immigration, empowered by adapted Christian symbols, and buffeted by a sense of racial superiority, the KKK saw themselves as a crusade to save America from internal and external threats. H.W. Evans, who became the Imperial Wizard of the Ku Klux Klan in 1922, stated his mission in these words: "As the Star of Bethlehem guided the wise men to Christ, so it is that the Klan is expected more and more to guide men to the right life under Christ's banner."

But is the fiery cross the banner of Christ? Is this what the cross truly means?

By the time a burning cross was placed on Martin Luther King, Jr.'s front lawn in 1960, the symbol had been used to intimidate and threaten thousands of minorities across America. Wherever a cross was burned, the saying went, a lynching was soon to follow. When Martin left his porch that morning, the world was watching through the lens of a newspaper reporter. How would he respond? Would he give up on his stance of non-violence and fight back? The cameraman captured the moment he pulled the cross from the ground. His face was calm, as if pulling a weed from his garden.

In a speech to the National Conference on Religion and Race, Dr. King referred to the cross, not the one in his yard but the one in his Bible. "The cross we bear precedes the crown we wear. To be a Christian one must take up his cross, with all of its difficulties and agonizing tension-packed content and carry it until that very cross leaves its mark upon us and redeems us to that more excellent way which comes only through suffering." Part of that suffering was forgiving those who sinned against him—answering hatred with love.

One preacher saw the cross as a fiery call to arms, the other saw it as a reason to forgive his enemies. One burned a cross on a hill to rally those like him to destroy those unlike him. The other looked to a different cross on a different hill where hatred and suffering gave way to love.

6.

Inclusive or Exclusive?

"Forgiveness flounders because I exclude the enemy from the community of humans even as I exclude myself from the community of sinners. But no one can be in the presence of the God of the crucified Messiah for long without overcoming this double exclusion—without transposing the enemy from the sphere of the monstrous . . . into the sphere of shared humanity and herself from the sphere of proud innocence into the sphere of common sinfulness. When one knows [as the cross demonstrates] that the torturer will not eternally triumph over the victim, one is free to rediscover that person's humanity and imitate God's love for him. And when one knows [as the cross demonstrates] that God's love is greater than all sin, one is free to see oneself in the light of God's justice and so rediscover one's own sinfulness."

—MIROSLAV VOLF

IN 1866, A BRITISH noble woman named Adeline Paulina Irby visited Sarajevo for the first time. She had been traveling in the region for three years and was moved to help the people she met. At that time, education was not widely available in Bosnia and Herzegovina. This was especially true for girls. Sarajevo did not have a bookstore, and there was only one other school for girls in the country. Adeline's dream was to train young women from the surrounding countryside as school teachers so they could return to teach others in their villages. She decided to open a school that would be free for all girls no matter their cultural, ethnic, or religious background.

In 1870 the school opened, and Adeline sent two young Protestant schoolteachers from Germany to run it. The school sat at the edge of town along the Miljacka River—a solid three-story building with a cross on top. The new school started with fanfare, however, only five girls registered to attend. The different cultural and religious groups in Sarajevo distrusted the school and its teachers. The difficulties continued for two more years until the Protestant deaconesses returned to Germany discouraged. Adeline was forced to move from England to oversee the school personally.

As she assessed the situation, she concluded some of the distrust was related to the cross. To certain citizens, the cross was a sign of exclusivity. It was like a stop sign saying, "Your kind are not welcome here!" This was ironic because the cross was the source of Adeline's humanitarian motivation. It was the meaning of the cross that led her to open the school in the first place. However, she was not willing to let the symbol of the cross distract from the meaning it symbolized. Adeline removed the cross from the roof of her school. Step-by-step she built trust with the community until the building was adorned with the smiling faces of 25 Bosnian children.

Those who charge the cross with exclusivity have reason to do so. Jesus made some exclusive statements. One such statement, reported in the Gospel of John, occurred while Jesus was sharing the Passover meal with his disciples the night before his crucifixion. John, who was sitting beside Jesus that evening, had a great vantage point to give us an inside look into this last supper. During the meal, Jesus said something that disturbed his friends. He said he would soon go away and they could not follow him. Distraught, Peter asked Jesus where he was going. Instead of answering Peter's question, Jesus reassured him that while they could not come with him now, they would follow afterwards. Peter, ever bold with his words, disagreed with Jesus' plan. He wanted to go with Jesus right away even if it meant giving up his life. But Jesus knew Peter was not as strong as he thought. He told Peter that before the morning dawned, Peter would deny him three times. Peter fell silent in disbelief.

Jesus returned to comforting his disciples. He told them he was going to his Father to prepare a place for them in his Father's house. He would come back again and take them so they could be with him. Then he added, mysteriously, "And you know the way to where I am going."

Thomas was the one who voiced the obvious question: "How can we know the way if we do not know where you are going?" I am sure any of us would have asked the same question. For accurate directions you need to know where you are and where you are going. If you do not know where you are going, how can you know how to get there? Thomas' question made sense. Jesus' answer was more surprising: "I am the way, and the truth, and the life. No one comes to the Father except through me."[1] Jesus, in essence, told his friends, "You don't have to know where you are going if you know Me."

This was an extremely exclusive statement. Some theologians try to "fix" Jesus' statement and make it less exclusive. "He really said, I am *a* way, *a* truth and *a* life." That would solve the problem, right? Except there is a clear definite article in the original language. This is also confirmed by the rest of Jesus' statement. He claims to be the only way to get to God. "No one" and "except through me" are exclusive phrases. Jesus is so central to getting to the Father, that the disciples didn't even need to know where they were going, as long as they had Jesus.

Jesus' exclusive message does not end with him; it continues in the writings of Paul. In his letter to the Galatians, Paul was concerned the Galatian believers would abandon the good news of Jesus, the gospel, for another "way." Religious teachers had come in among these believers and tried to convince them that Jesus was not enough to get to the Father. According to these teachers, the Galatians also needed to follow certain religious traditions. Paul was aggressively exclusive at the beginning of his letter: "I am astonished that you are so quickly deserting him who called you in the grace of Christ and are turning to a different gospel—not that there is another one . . . "[2]

This gospel Paul was protecting is the "gospel of Christ"—the assertion that he is the way, the truth, and the life. Paul went on to make a pretty dramatic statement about the exclusivity of this gospel. "But even if we or an angel from heaven should preach to you a gospel contrary to the one we preached to you, let him be accursed."[3] According to Paul, even if a heavenly being appears to you with a contrary message, it is not true. Then, just to ensure the Galatians got his point, Paul repeated this statement in the next verse.

According to Jesus and Paul, the message of the Bible is exclusive. This means that the cross is exclusive as well. This exclusivity offends modern sensibilities. Inclusivity is perhaps the highest value of this generation. The

1. John 14:6
2. Galatians 1:6–7
3. Galatians 1:8

great wrong of modern society is to say someone else is wrong. Sometimes this is expressed as, "Who are you to say that you are right and he is wrong?" This idea extends to all aspects of life.

The idea of religious inclusivity is not a new one. Six hundred years ago, the Japanese Zen Buddhist poet Ikkyu said, "Many paths lead from the foot of the mountain, but at the peak we all gaze at the single bright moon." This is paraphrased today as, "Many paths lead to the top of the mountain." We can all walk our own paths and still get to God. No religion has to be "right" because we can all be "right." This concept sounds noble to our modern ears, but where does this leave the cross and Jesus who claimed to be the only way?

There is a major problem with the mountain path metaphor: mountains are difficult to climb. For example, few of us will ever make it to the top of Mount Everest. Reaching the top of Everest takes tremendous physical ability. You train for at least a year, running, lifting weights, carrying a fifty pound pack on eight-hour hikes. To climb Everest to the summit, you must be in peak physical shape. The altitude, the lack of oxygen, the danger (four out of a hundred people die) all take a toll. If you have a health issue, or a significant disability or limitation, the mountain is not for you.

All this preparation takes time. The people who succeed in reaching Everest's summit have enough expendable time to train, to travel around the world, to take two months off work to climb. How many people in the world have that much time? And what about the costs? It can cost around $100,000 to summit Everest. The permit fees for climbing are equal to the price of a car. Hiring a guide is the cost of another luxury car. This again puts the summit out of reach for those who don't have that kind of money.

This means, while there is more than one path to the top of Everest, only those with certain physical and financial advantages can ever hope to reach the top. This is Everest, the highest mountain on earth. How high is the mountain where we can meet God?

There is something subtly exclusive about the "many paths lead to the summit" idea. There is a tremendous advantage to those born into families where faith and character are important. What about those who have been rejected by society by wrong deeds they have done or wrong deeds done against them? What about those entangled in addictions or relationships or bad habits? Are they excluded from the mountaintop because they are unable to climb?

The religious Everest climbers of Jesus' day were the Pharisees. They prayed more than anyone else. They dedicated more time to God than anyone else. They gave more money to God than anyone else. They kept detailed lists of rules to ensure they were obeying God's law completely. From their exalted position as religious leaders, they looked down on those who were unable to make the climb.

How did Jesus react to these Pharisees? He called them snakes. He said they were gleaming tombstones, white on the outside but full of dried bones. He said they were people who washed only the outside of their cups while ignoring the residue inside. Jesus was against the Pharisees, and the Pharisees were against Jesus.

Instead of gathering around Him the religious elites, Jesus surrounded Himself with "sinners" and outcasts. Once, when Jesus was invited into the home of one of these Pharisees, a woman who was known as the town "sinner," broke into the dinner party and began to wash Jesus' feet with her hair and tears. As she kissed Jesus' dirty feet and poured oil over them, the host was shocked. He thought, "A truly religious man would never allow a woman like that to touch Him. If Jesus were a prophet, He would know what kind of woman she was and rebuke her." Instead of rebuking the woman, Jesus rebuked His host. As for the woman, the one who was not allowed into polite society because of her past, He forgave her.

As we compare Jesus with the Pharisees we must ask, "Who is exclusive and who is inclusive?" Inclusivity is, by definition, "an intention of including people who might otherwise be excluded or marginalized." The excluded and marginalized were exactly the people with whom Jesus surrounded Himself. He welcomed the outcast leper, the sinful adulteress, the traitorous tax collector, and the violent zealot. Even though He claimed to be the only way to the Father, it was a diverse crowd that passed along that way. His call was an inclusive one. He said, "Come to me, all who labor and are heavy laden, and I will give you rest. Take my yoke upon you, and learn from me, for I am gentle and lowly in heart, and you will find rest for your souls. For my yoke is easy, and my burden is light."[4] Jesus didn't round up the best climbers to join His climbing club. He called the excluded and marginalized, weighed down by the past, present, and future, to find rest in Him.

4. Matthew 11:28–30

It is helpful to recognize there is more than one type of exclusivity and inclusivity. There is actually a type of exclusivity we all affirm and support. Imagine that the world is overtaken by a plague and every inhabitant is infected. The plague is quick and effective—every person who contracts it dies. Just when all hope seems lost, news breaks that a scientist has discovered a cure for the disease. Celebrations break out around the globe in honor of the drug maker. Headlines read, "Miracle cure found!" Humankind is saved. Embedded in this short story is an exclusive claim: the only way to be saved from death is to take this drug. If the statement is true, if the drug works, it is the good kind of exclusive. We are comfortable with this kind of exclusivity. In fact, it would be dangerous to say, "You can take any drug you want and still get better." Such a statement would result in death.

However, there is another kind of exclusivity. Imagine the day after the drug is revealed a second news bulletin is released. The maker of the drug will only share the cure with people who are of his same ethnic background or who can afford to pay a billion dollars for the pill. Panic ensues and the drug maker is vilified in every country on earth, except his own. This added information reveals a second type of exclusivity, the kind we loathe. This exclusivity is prejudiced and closed-minded. It is spiteful and mean. And it is completely unlike Jesus and the cross.

The Apostle Paul was a Pharisee before he became a follower of Jesus. If anyone could summit the religious Everest in his community, it was Paul. He was not only a Jew, like Moses, he was trained by the most famous Jewish teacher of his age. He was not only a Pharisee, he was one of the most zealous of the Pharisees. He was not only a free man, he was a Roman citizen. The doors of the Roman world were open to him because of it. Unlike a slave, he could travel freely and speak openly. He was the beneficiary of every advantage of the age.

But an encounter with Jesus changed everything for Paul. He began to see things through the inclusive lens of the cross. He wrote, "There is neither Jew nor Greek, there is neither slave nor free, there is no male and female, for you are all one in Christ Jesus."[5] No longer was he looking down the mountain at those below him, he was looking up at Jesus and that changed the way he looked at those around him. No longer did Paul take pride in his citizenship, or his sex, or his religious upbringing. All that was garbage to him compared to knowing Jesus. His new object of pride was the

5. Galatians 3:28

cross. "But far be it from me to boast except in the cross of our Lord Jesus Christ, by which the world has been crucified to me, and I to the world."[6]

Why would Paul boast in the cross, this symbol that is so often rejected? Because the cross opens the way for everyone, no matter their social status, religious achievements, ethnic background, or sex. The cross stands opposed to our efforts to climb the mountain to God. The message of the cross is, "You can't do it yourself. You need help." There, in our need, we are all on the same footing. It is not, "we are all okay," but "we are all not okay." And no advantage can overcome the fact that we need supernatural help to reach God.

The cross is not a stop sign declaring, "Your kind are not welcome here." It is a beacon calling all who are weary and heavy laden to find rest. The biggest problem with trying to climb to God is that God is not at the top of the mountain. In Jesus, he descended the mountain. At the cross God stooped down. There, in the dark and dirty valley of our world, he opened a way for the excluded of society to find inclusion in him.

6. Galatians 6:14

7.

Refugee Days

"Meeting the needs of the world's displaced people—both refugees and the internally displaced—is much more complex than simply providing short-term security and assistance. It is about addressing the persecution, violence and conflict which bring about displacement in the first place. It is about recognizing the human rights of all men, women and children to enjoy peace, security and dignity without having to flee their homes."

—THE STATE OF THE WORLD'S REFUGEES 2000

IN THE SPRING OF 1992, a story spread among the BiH refugees in Serbia that men aged sixteen to sixty needed permission from the military to leave the country. There was no way for me to get this confirmation because I was certain if I showed up at a military base, I would quickly find myself drafted and sent to the front line in BiH. I heard a lot of stories of how the police were organizing raids in the city, going into cafes or stopping buses to check everyone's paperwork. Military-aged men whose documents showed a residence in Bosnia and Herzegovina were immediately taken and driven to the military barracks in Bubanj Potok where they received a uniform and urgent orders to return to the front. They couldn't even telephone their families.

That was the first problem, but there was a second one as well: if we left, where would we go? My cousin's husband, in whose apartment we lived, moved to Cyprus and started a business because of the large tax relief Cyprus gave to foreign investors. After my mother decided to go with my nephew and niece through Hungary to my sister in Croatia, my cousin in

Cyprus invited Sanja and me to come and stay with them. Because there was a high probability the police at the airport would arrest me and hand me over to military authorities instead of allowing me to cross the border, we decided that Sanja would come on the next flight if I succeeded in crossing the border. However, if I was taken and mobilized, then she would try to get to Croatia with my mother, where Sanja's parents were at that moment, and I would try to contact them later when the situation calmed down. We had no idea that the situation would not calm down, but, instead, would intensify through the next three years.

Those few days before the trip, after buying my plane ticket, I prayed secretly every night. The trip arrived only one day after my 23rd birthday, May 20, 1992. I said goodbye to my mother and my nephew and niece, not knowing I wouldn't see them again for more than three years, and headed to the airport with Sanja and Oleg, who had also escaped to Belgrade. After saying goodbye to them, I headed towards the border police counter. I handed him my ticket and passport. He looked at them for some time, then glanced up at me and asked if I had clearance from the military. Fearfully, I answered that I didn't. After a moment of short consideration, he waved his hand, gave me back my passport and ticket, and motioned that I could pass. Overjoyed, I turned around and waved once more to Sanja and Oleg and then headed toward the gate.

The flight lasted two-and-a-half hours. An older man from Serbia, who was going to Cyprus for vacation, sat next to me. While he talked to me of his travels and his vacations, my head was filled with nightmarish images. I couldn't believe we were traveling from the same country; I was escaping a war and he was going on vacation. After landing at the airport in Larnaca, a Cypriot police officer started questioning me: where will I stay, why don't I have a hotel reservation, how much money do I have with me, and on and on. I told him I had a large sum of money and he asked to see it. I had hidden the money in different places in my luggage and it took me awhile to find it all because I had forgotten where I had put it. Finally, the policeman let me go—the other passengers had left ages ago—and I found my very worried cousin and her husband waiting for me outside.

Upon my arrival in Cyprus, things became a little clearer. Cyprus had a civil war in the middle of the 1970s which divided it into two parts and, twenty years after the war, the southern half still officially had "refugees" from the northern part of the island. Due to this, according to international law, they weren't obligated to accept refugees from other countries caught in war. I couldn't get refugee status and could only stay as a guest with my cousin and her husband, who had business visas, for a maximum of three months. Even then, I had to report every month to the immigration office so they could consider my application, approve my stay for another month, or deport me. The only way I could legally stay in Cyprus was to get a job and a work visa. The problem was that Sanja wasn't related to my cousins so she couldn't come as their guests.

Only ten days after my arrival in Cyprus, the UN voted for Resolution 757 in which economic sanctions were leveled against Yugoslavia—all civilian flights to and from Yugoslavia were banned. The media started speculating about a possible NATO bombing of Yugoslavia. My mother obtained passports from the Red Cross for my niece and nephew and prepared to pass through Hungary to Croatia, to my sister in Makarska. I was safe in Cyprus, but Sanja was supposed to stay alone in Belgrade facing sanctions and the threat of bombs.

I put all my energy into finding a solution to bring Sanja to Cyprus, while, in the meantime, we agreed she should travel to Skopje, Macedonia to stay with a long-time friend of my mom's and to wait there for things to develop. We hired my cousin's attorneys in Cyprus and, after a consultation with them, discovered we needed to find Sanja a job and apply for a work visa because that was the only way she could come and stay in Cyprus. The problem was that the whole process could last up to three months, and we were in a hurry.

The prayers I prayed earlier in Mostar and in Belgrade had brought about a great change in me, although it couldn't be seen from the outside—from a diehard atheist, I had become an agnostic. I was no longer certain that God did not exist, and, to the contrary, I saw that my prayers brought inner peace and helped with my problems in a way I couldn't understand. Once again there was a problem before me I couldn't solve; once again I prayed. This time I prayed for God to find a way for Sanja to come to Cyprus. I prayed every night. After a few days, a doctor contacted us—a Cypriot and gynecologist who was the owner of a small private clinic. He heard I was looking for a job for my girlfriend and he needed a worker in the birthing center immediately.

It wasn't a problem that Sanja had graduated from an electro-technical high school, and not a medical one, because they needed someone to maintain the building and help the mothers before and after birth. They had an agreement with a girl from Sarajevo who was supposed to come work for them and they had finished the whole application process and administrative red tape for her, but because of the war in Bosnia and Herzegovina they lost contact. After waiting for some time to see if she would contact them, they heard I was looking for work for Sanja and contacted me. They had some contacts in the Immigration Office who could expedite the whole process, and Sanja came to Cyprus in a couple of weeks—one more answered prayer.

The next two months flew by, Sanja worked in the clinic and I worked a few temporary black-market jobs. I started to work at a car wash. Even though gambling was outlawed in Cyprus, I heard there was a gambling house with machines on a foreign military base. I was able to get in contact with the Cypriot who was the owner of the machines, and I offered to work for him. He hired me for a probationary period. As soon as I started working, I saw that his workers were stealing from him. The workers realized I had more experience and knowledge than they did and felt threatened. They lied about me to the boss, and he didn't hire me. I couldn't renew my tourist visa, but I found another job in a fast food restaurant. At that time, I had to leave Cyprus and remain out of the country for a few weeks to finish the work visa process.

Because of the international embargo and sanctions, Yugoslavia (at that time Serbia and Montenegro) officially dissociated itself from the war in Bosnia and Herzegovina, and therefore discontinued drafting and returning refugees to BiH. I was in contact with Oleg and some other friends, and they assured me I could travel freely, since there was no longer forced mobilization. An embargo on flights was still in place, however, so I was forced to fly to Sofia, Bulgaria and travel by bus to Belgrade, where I waited for the completion of the visa process. After a couple of weeks, I received my visa, and returned to Cyprus via Sofia to Larnaca to begin work. Sanja and I both worked two jobs and sent money to relatives in Mostar and to Sanja's brother, who was studying in Zagreb.

In the meantime, after several months of conflict and shelling in Mostar, the Serbian Army encircling Mostar retreated, and the fighting and shelling stopped. My mother, sister, nephew, niece, and Sanja's parents returned to Mostar from Makarska to their homes (which were damaged from shelling), and continued with a fairly normal life. Those few months as refugees in Makarska were difficult ones. Even though my grandma and aunt (my mother's mom and sister) lived in Makarska, they hadn't really welcomed my mother and sister who, in the end, had to seek lodging in a collective refugee center. Circumstances were complicated because my sister's married name accentuated the fact that her husband was a Serb.

As soon as the situation in Mostar calmed down a bit, they returned home. Even though the phone lines in their apartments were not working, we found a way to talk with them on the phone sometimes, and letters started regularly arriving by mail. This was before e-mail, internet, social media, so letters were the only way to communicate. Sanja's father started working on the power substations where there was a telephone and a few times we succeeded in talking, if only briefly.

Life in Mostar slowly normalized and we were happy to help them a little financially, even if sending money wasn't simple. We sent money and letters to friends in Germany, who sent them on to Mostar through people they knew. Their letters were coming back to us the same way. Letters could be sent through the Red Cross, but normal postal service with Mostar was still not functional. After the retreat of the Serbian Army from Mostar, Croats and Bosniaks lived there together in peace for several months.

On May 9, 1993, intense conflicts started between the Army of the Republic of Bosnia and Herzegovina and the Croatian Defense Council (HVO) in Mostar. Those conflicts continued until the end of the war. The city was divided into two parts. The front line was established on the north, it went down by the Neretva River to the Carinski Bridge, then it followed Šantićeva Street to the Old Gymnasium (high school), and then along the Boulevard to the south. There was intense fighting, shelling, killing, arrests, and persecution. Again, the front line was only a few hundred meters from our building and the apartment where my mother now lived alone. All telephone lines were disconnected and from that day forward, letters stopped arriving. We lost all contact with our loved ones in Mostar. All the information we received about home was from the media—newspaper articles and TV news—through which we watched the battles and destruction. Those were hard days for us; we feared for the fate of our loved ones.

8.

The Red Cross

"Imperturbable, unwearying, unfaltering, their quiet self-sacrifice made little of fatigue and horrors, and of their own devotion."

—HENRI DUNANT, FOUNDER OF THE RED CROSS, WRITING OF THE VOLUNTEERS WHO TENDED THE WOUNDED AT THE BATTLE OF SOLFERINO

HENRI DUNANT RUSHES INTO a church outside of Solferino, Italy, that has been transformed into a makeshift hospital. Wounded French and Austrian soldiers cover the floor as moaning fills the air. Dunant is not a doctor. He is a Swiss businessman who, days earlier, happened upon the largest European battle in fifty years. With more than 40,000 soldiers killed or wounded in the battle, Dunant decided to help organize the local townspeople in caring for the helpless men. He is rushing into the church because he has figured out a solution to their biggest problem. Even though the surrounding towns are already full of dying men, there are thousands more suffering on the battlefield. But how can the townspeople reach them without ending up wounded themselves?

Dunant grabs a length of white cloth and lays it out on the floor of the church. He dips a rag into a pan of blood from the surgery table and spreads it onto the material in the shape of a cross. "A red cross," he says, attaching the banner to a wooden pole. "A cross of blood is our flag!" The men cheer as he waves his flag before them.

The townspeople gather outside on horses and in wagons, each draped with the new symbol of their cause—the red cross. With Dunant leading on horseback, they march out into the ongoing battle. He leads the procession directly between the French and Austrian front lines. At first, the French captain does not know what to do—the two armies continue firing at one another. However, as Dunant reaches the battlefield, his white flag with the red cross waving in the wind, the captain orders his men to hold their fire. When the Austrian captain does the same, the townspeople place the wounded men on stretchers and remove them from danger. As the scene fades, both armies rise to their feet and salute the brave men and women bearing the cross of blood. It is a picture of humanity in the midst of inhumanity.

The founding of the Red Cross was much less dramatic than the above version, fictionalized for the film "Henri Dunant: Red on the Cross." However, it does capture the radical changes Henri Dunant set into motion. Is there anything more dehumanizing than war? And yet, in the midst of war was born one of the world's greatest humanitarian pursuits. And all under the banner of the cross.

Henri Dunant was raised in Geneva during a period of spiritual awakening in the first half of the 19th century. His family traced their religious heritage to the Protestant Reformation and John Calvin, a preacher, leader, and reformer in Geneva during the 16th century. When Henri turned eighteen, he joined the Geneva Society for Alms Giving and spent much of his free time visiting prisons and organizing humanitarian work. He and his friends, who met each Thursday to study the Bible and help the poor, became known as the "Thursday Association." In his twenties, he founded the Geneva chapter of the Young Men's Christian Association (YMCA) which sought to put Christian principles into practice by helping young men develop a healthy "body, mind, and spirit." Three years later he convinced the other chapters of the YMCA to form a truly global movement, initiating the first international conference in Paris. Young Henri's life was defined by faith and social endeavors.

In 1856, a year after the YMCA conference in Paris, Dunant began a business to grow and trade corn in French-controlled Algeria. It was this business that brought him to the fateful events in Solferino. Although he had received a land grant for his company in Algeria, the water rights were not clearly designated and the local officials would not allow him to access necessary water supplies. He decided to appeal directly to Napoleon III, Emperor of France, who was, at the time, with his army in northern Italy preparing to support Piedmont-Sardinia in their bid for independence from Austria. He arrived at the French headquarters the evening of June 24, 1859, to find "the most dreadful sights imaginable. Bodies of men and horses covered the battlefield; corpses were strewn over roads, ditches, ravines, thickets and fields; the approaches of Solferino were literally thick with the dead. The fields were devastated, wheat and corn lying flat on the ground, fences broken, orchards ruined; here and there were pools of blood." That day the two armies, numbering more than 300,000, had fought for fifteen hours. The battle lines stretched for twelve miles. "Everywhere men fell by thousands, with gaping wounds in limbs or bellies, riddled with bullets, mortally wounded by shot and shell of every kind." It took three days to bury the dead on the battlefield, while bodies were found hidden in ditches and under bushes for the next three weeks. The local townspeople gathered to provide aid to the wounded and the village of Castiglione became a makeshift hospital. It was there that Dunant made his presence felt.

As Dunant would later recount, "I sought to organize as best I could relief in the quarters where it seemed to be most lacking, and I adopted in particular one of the Castiglione churches . . . Nearly 500 soldiers were there, piled in the church, and a hundred more lay on straw in front of the church . . . Men of all nations lay side by side on the flagstone floor . . . Frenchmen and Arabs, Germans and Slavs . . . Oaths, curses and cries such as no words can describe resounded from the vaulting of the sacred buildings." Though not trained medically, Dunant and the villagers gave water to the suffering soldiers, bandaged their wounds, and recorded letters to send back to their homes. They made no distinction between nationalities or allegiances. The women of Castiglione simple said "tutti fratelli," ("All are brothers") and continued their "imperturbable, unwearying, unfaltering, quiet self-sacrifice."

In all, over 40,000 men were killed or wounded on June 24. Three years after the battle, Henri Dunant published a record of the events in his book *The Battle of Solferino* in which he describes, in gruesome detail, the reality for these wounded soldiers. In one of his footnotes, buried on page 73, he makes a suggestion that would soon echo around the world: "If these pages could bring up the questions . . . of the help to be given to wounded soldiers in wartime, or of the first aid to be afforded them after an engagement . . . I shall have fully attained my goal." He later expands on the improvements he hoped for. "There is need, therefore, for voluntary orderlies and volunteer nurses, zealous, trained and experienced, whose position would be recognized by the commanders or armies in the field, and their mission facilitated and supported." The best way to organize these changes, according to Dunant, was to bring together government leaders during a time of peace. "On certain occasions, as, for example, when princes of the military art belonging to different nationalities meet at Cologne or Chalons, would it not be desirable that they should take advantage of this sort of congress to formulate some international principle, sanctioned by a Convention inviolate in character, which, once agreed upon and ratified, might constitute the basis for societies for the relief of the wounded in the different European countries?"

These suggestions sound obvious to us today in an age of the United Nations, however, in Dunant's time, when the machines of war were advancing faster than the rule of law, they were revolutionary. For Dunant, it was not only revolutionary, it was imperative. "Humanity and civilization call imperiously for such an organization as is here suggested . . . In an age when we hear so much of progress and civilization, is it not a matter of urgency, since unhappily we cannot always avoid wars, to press forward in a human and truly civilized spirit the attempt to prevent, or at least to alleviate, the horrors of war?"

On February 17, 1863, less than a year after the publication of *The Battle of Solferino*, Dunant and four leading men of Geneva met to pursue implementing Dunant's suggestions. This meeting is viewed as the founding of the International Committee of the Red Cross. A year later the Swiss parliament organized a gathering of sixteen nations to discuss the treatment of the wounded in wartime. The result of the conference was the signing of the first Geneva Convention "for the Amelioration of the Condition of the Wounded and Sick in Armed Forces in the Field." Twelve nations signed what has now become the international standard for humanitarian treatment in war. It was at this first Geneva Convention that a neutral symbol was chosen to mark nurses and doctors tending to the sick and wounded. The symbol had to be distinct, neutral, and uniform between countries. The conference chose for that global symbol a red cross on a white background.

Clara Barton, the founder of the American Branch of the Red Cross, wrote forty years after the Geneva Convention, "From the first filaments spun in the heart of a solitary traveler have been drawn onward stronger and larger strands, until now more than forty of the principal nations of the earth are bound together by bonds of the highest international law, that must make war in the future less barbarous than it has been in the past." In 1901, Dunant was recognized for his contribution, when he received the first Nobel Peace Prize. Today, the organization is in 190 nations and present on almost every battlefield around the globe. Imagine the elation felt by the wounded soldier, left to die on the field of battle, when his eye catches the white flag with a red cross coming toward him. Could this be a picture of the true meaning of the cross?

One of the goals of the first Geneva Convention was to create one symbol, common among all nations, that would set apart medical staff as neutral participants on the battlefield. However, as we have already seen, the cross is a powerful symbol. Over the past 150 years, the most intense discussions within the Red Cross have been related to the symbol of the cross. During the Russo-Turkish War from 1877–1878, the Ottoman Empire, a signer of the Geneva Convention, unilaterally declared it would be using a red crescent on a white field to mark its ambulances because the cross had "so far prevented Turkey from exercising its rights under the Convention because it gave offense to Muslim soldiers." Iran later refused to use the cross or the crescent in protest to both the West and the Ottoman Empire, preferring a red lion. While the Red Cross accepted the Red Crescent as an international symbol of their organization, the argument has continued into this century. In 2005, the red diamond (a symbol completely devoid of any religious symbolism) was added to the cross and crescent as an international symbol of the Red Cross.

The cross is such a powerful symbol it can be offensive even in doing good. Can the cross be emptied of its religious meaning? Should it be? As we have seen so far, history cloaks the true meaning of the cross. Unfortunately, doctors and nurses are not the only ones who have marched into battle under the sign of the cross.

9

Necessary or Unnecessary?

"Outside of the cross of Jesus Christ, there is no hope in this world. That cross and resurrection at the core of the Gospel is the only hope for humanity. Wherever you go, ask God for wisdom on how to get that Gospel in, even in the toughest situations of life."

—RAVI ZACHARIAS

VLADO LIVED IN BELGRADE on a fairly quiet street. He had a relatively new VW Passat that he parked on the sidewalk in front of his house every evening. One morning he woke up, drank some coffee, left his house to go to work . . . and his car wasn't there. While he was trying to figure out what happened, his phone rang. The voice on the line informed him that they had stolen his car and if he reported the theft to the police, he would never see his car again because they would rip it apart and sell the parts. However, if he paid them a fourth of the value, he would get the car back. Vlado was a salesman so he started to haggle, telling them the car wasn't worth as much as they were asking. When they agreed on a price he was willing to pay, Vlado wanted to ensure that all of his things, especially his expensive CD player, were still in the car. The thief on the phone said everything was still inside and, in answer to Vlado's question how could he be sure that after he paid the money he would get his car back with all his things, the thief replied, "Well, I'm an honorable man. I won't lie to you!"

A thief, an honorable man? What standard did he use to measure his honor? And what standard do you and I use to measure ours? Are we honorable people and what connection does this have to the cross? The Bible teaches us that God created the whole universe, including this world in which we live. You can read about this in the first chapter of the the first book of the Bible, Genesis. After creating the heavens and the earth, light and water, plants and animals, God created man and woman in His image, and "God saw everything that he had made, and behold, it was very good."[1] God placed man in the Garden of Eden to take care of it, to farm it, and protect it. He allowed him to eat of every tree in the garden, except for the one tree from which he commanded him not to eat.[2]

What happens when you tell a child, "You can play with all the toys, but don't touch this one"? What happens when you tell adults, "You can go in every room, but just don't go in this one"? "Forbidden fruit" often attracts us, and that's part of our fallen, sinful nature. The first man and woman couldn't resist temptation; they did exactly what God told them not to do and suffered the consequences. Disobedience to God's commandments is called sin. It is not just about disobeying His commandments but about disobeying the One who gave these commandments, about disobeying the Creator who loves us, about disobeying God.

Let me try to illustrate: imagine a teenage driver, eighteen years old, who is caught running a red light and brought before a judge. We would say he needs to be punished because he broke the law. But, imagine that the judge is his father, who gave him the car and asked him to drive carefully and pay attention to red lights. Now this changes the situation. It is not just about breaking the law, but breaking a relationship. All people, including you and me, tend toward sin and bear the consequences for it. God is holy and righteous, He takes disobedience of His commands personally, so no sin can stand in His presence. That means the first and greatest consequence of sin is separation from God.

But we bear other consequences as well. God didn't give us commandments in the Bible to steal our fun, like some people think, but to protect us from the consequences of sin. You lie to someone, and that person finds out, you lose their trust. You steal and you can end up in jail. You commit adultery and your family falls apart—your kids grow up without a mother or a father. You don't forgive and bitterness grows in your heart—a bitterness that eats you from the inside. You get drunk and cause a car accident where you hurt yourself and others. You steal a car and hold it for ransom

1. Genesis 1:31
2. Genesis 2

and ask the owner to buy it back, yet still think you are an honorable man. The list of sins and consequences is too long to fit in this book! The consequences are frightening: separation from God in eternity as well as suffering in this life, "For the wages of sin is death."[3] That wasn't God's plan for this world. But is God's supernatural intervention truly necessary for us? Maybe it's necessary for someone else, someone worse, but not for me, we will probably say, "Because I am an honorable man."

When we think about honor and respect, about whether we are good or bad, often we put people in categories—good, bad, or ugly—like the Sergio Leone film. Which category am I in? Where's the line between good and evil? Usually, we put that line "beneath our feet"—everyone worse than me is really bad, sinful, and rotten, and I, well I am good and honorable. If I lie, at least I didn't steal anything. If I steal, at least I didn't kill anyone. If I kill, I had a reason. If I am envious, I should be. If I am jealous, others are to blame . . . everyone is to blame except me. I'm just right, honorable and respectable.

Aleksandr Solzhenitsyn, the Russian writer and philosopher who spent eight years in Siberia in Stalin's Gulag wrote, "Gradually it was disclosed to me that the line separating good and evil passes not through states, nor between classes, nor between political parties either—but right through every human heart—and through all human hearts . . . even within hearts overwhelmed by evil, one small bridgehead of good is retained. And even in the best of all hearts, there remains . . . an un-uprooted small corner of evil." And that's exactly our problem, an un-uprooted corner of evil exists in every one of our hearts. In the Bible it says, "For all have sinned and fall short of the glory of God."[4]

But God decided to intervene and give man another chance. Through the Old Testament we can see the establishment of a system of animal sacrifices. You can read about this in the first chapter of the third book of the Bible, Leviticus, as well as in many other Old Testament books. People would recognize their sins, repent for them, and then, as a sign of their repentance and desire to change, bring a sacrifice. The sacrificial lamb paid for the person's sins with its life. In the New Testament, in the letter to the Hebrews,[5] it is written that those animal sacrifices, which were brought over and over again, were imperfect and could not "cleanse" sin. They only

3. Romans 6:23

4. Romans 3:23

5. Hebrews 10

reminded people that they were sinful and that sin has consequences. Then what's the solution? How can people be helped to solve the problem of sin? God decided to do something revolutionary, something unfathomable, something unique.

Some two thousand years ago in Israel there lived a young girl, a teenager, named Mary. She was engaged to a carpenter, a young man named Joseph, whom she was supposed to marry. She was a virgin because they kept themselves for the wedding night. One day an angel appeared to Mary and told her that, even though she was a virgin, she would become pregnant by the power of the Holy Spirit and would conceive supernaturally. Then the angel appeared to Joseph in a dream and informed him of the events that would transpire. He told them to call their son Emmanuel, *Yeshua* (Jesus), which means, "God with us," "God saves." Everything happened just as the angel described. Jesus was born. Even as a baby they persecuted him and tried to kill Him, and He had to go with His parents into exile. We read about all this in the New Testament in the first chapters of the gospels.

When Jesus grew up, the time came for Him to fulfill the mission for which He came, the mission by which He received the name "God saves." God didn't need just to be born and live like one of us, He needed to die, to pay the price with His life for our sins. He needed to go to the cross, an instrument used for torturing criminals, and on that cross be tortured. Why? To save me and you? God Himself came into this world the same way we come into the world. He "placed" Himself in a woman's womb and was born just like us, except without sin. This is something that is unfathomable and unthinkable to us, and God planned it even before the creation of the world. The Old Testament has at least 365 prophecies about Jesus, at least one for every day of the year. The first prophecy is found in the third chapter of Genesis. Then in almost every book of the Old Testament we find prophecies about Jesus. Why then is it so hard for us to not only accept that it happened but also to understand it? Why is the cross, and the idea of the cross so offensive to so many people? If this is really the truth, why is it so hard for me to accept the cross as a symbol of something necessary—necessary for me and my good?

A few years before the cross, Jesus started His public work. He said that the time had come, that the Kingdom of God was at hand, in our grasp, and that people needed to become aware of sin and its consequences and decide to change. One day He entered a synagogue and, during the service, he started reading the prophecy of the prophet Isaiah, a prophecy about Himself, "The Spirit of the Lord is upon me, because he has anointed me to proclaim good news to the poor. He has sent me to proclaim liberty to the captives and recovering of sight to the blind, to set at liberty those who are oppressed, to proclaim the year of the Lord's favor."[6] What was Isaiah talking about? Why did Jesus read it, and even stranger why did He stop mid-sentence? Because the continuation of Isaiah's prophecy says that Jesus came also to proclaim the day of vengeance of our God.[7]

According to the dictionary, vengeance is "the brutal, disproportional revenge of the stronger side." God is definitely the stronger side, and for sin (disobedience to His commandments) we face not only consequences in this life but also vengeance that follows us into eternity. Jesus came to break this pattern, so that people, despite their sins, don't have to experience vengeance. The quote Jesus read in the synagogue that day when He spoke of the captive, the blind, and the oppressed doesn't just refer to the physically captive, the physically blind and the physically oppressed. We can be spiritually captive, blind, and oppressed.

The eighth chapter of the letter to the Romans speaks about how sin keeps us in bondage and leads to death. A captive doesn't have his own free will, and so, when we are in bondage to sin, we don't have a free will, we serve sin, and we can't get free. Spiritual captivity is worse than physical captivity. When we are in bondage to sin, we are often blind to our own sin. We see the sins of other people, but we don't see our own, or our sins seem really small compared to the sins of others. This is how a person who steals someone's car can say about himself, "I'm an honorable man." A blind man can stumble and fall, but the spiritually blind are in much more danger than the physically blind.

Many in the world today are oppressed and disenfranchised, without the opportunity to choose. Sin causes our oppression, taking away all our rights except the right to suffer and to make others suffer, taking away our choice. Jesus came to break that vicious cycle. The penalty for sin is death, and the consequences of sin are life's oppression and God's vengeance. Jesus came to give His life to pay the penalty for our sin, to be the perfect sacrifice, and to take the vengeance and wrath of God upon Himself . . . for me . . . and for you . . . because of His love for us! Is there another solution? No! We can't help ourselves! Was the cross necessary? Was it necessary for the

6. Luke 4:18–19

7. Isaiah 61:1–2

man who stole Vlado's car and thinks he's honorable? Was it necessary for me? And you? I believe if you continue reading to the end of this book, you will find the answer to these questions. If the cross wasn't necessary, why did all of this happen, and if it was necessary, why is it so hard for people to understand and accept?

10.

Signs and Wonders

"Miracles are not contrary to nature but only contrary
to what we know about nature."
—AUGUSTINE OF HIPPO

AFTER SANJA ARRIVED IN Cyprus and the situation in Mostar calmed down, I forgot about God. I didn't need Him anymore. I forgot about all those promises I made to Him when I prayed. Life was again under my control. But then theworries and problemsreturned—anxiety for my mother, sister, her family, and Sanja's parents . . . we didn't know if they were alive or dead. So again, I started praying. I prayed that God would keep them safe and that they would survive the war. A few years later, when we met for the first time after the war in a village called Berkovići on the dividing line in Herzegovina, I saw how God answered that prayer. I prayed every night in secret, even Sanja didn't know I was praying. I had considered prayer a sign of weakness, so I didn't want anyone to know that I was praying. On the outside I continued to play the atheist, but deep inside something was changing.

In Mostar, June 1993, in the heat of war, my sister gave birth to a beautiful baby girl. Because of the stress caused by daily fearing for her life, she wasn't able to produce enough milk to nurse, and there wasn't any baby food (nor did she have electricity, water, or diapers). My brother-in-law went to a humanitarian aid organization in Mostar to find help. They received him nicely, but when they heard his last name and saw his nation-ality they apologized and said that unfortunately they didn't have enough for everyone—they only helped "their own" people. He went to another aid organization and the same story repeated itself. Unfortunately, he was a minority in town, and "his" nationality was the enemy. Then my mother heard about Agape, a humanitarian aid organization of the Evangelical Church. She thought it was worth a try, so she went and sought help. Pastor Nikola, who received her and listened to her, asked to see the child's birth certificate. Mom thought the story would repeat a third time when he saw the father's name on the birth certificate, but he only wanted to see that the baby existed and that the items wouldn't end up at the marketplace. He gave my mom baby food, diapers, and some other necessities, and told her to come again when she ran out of food and he would see if he could help her again. He also invited her to the church service they held on Sundays.

The first Sunday she went out of gratitude, and maybe to leave a good impression so she could continue receiving aid. But in that service, something happened and God touched her. That wasn't the first time my mom had heard about the Good News of Jesus. A couple of years before the war, while returning home on a bus from Split where I served in the military, a man stood up in the bus, opened a Bible, and started speaking about Jesus. She said this left an impression and afterwards she thought about it a lot.

When the situation in Mostar normalized a little, letters started arriving. We were overjoyed. In the first letter, my mom wrote about life in Mostar and it was full of comments about God, Jesus, the Bible, etc. Because my mom was a communist and an atheist, I thought she was a little "touched in the head" because of the shelling. Later I discovered that she wasn't "touched" in the way I thought; she had been touched by the true meaning of the cross.

In July 1994, Sanja and I were married. At our wedding, there were about 50 of us: my cousins, our coworkers, and our friends we had met in Cyprus. We were married in City Hall and, in the evening, we had a reception in the restaurant where I worked. My cousin, Kristina, was the maid of honor, and the son of the restaurant owner Georgios, the best man. In war-torn Mostar, my mom and a couple of friends gathered together at Sanja's parents and modestly celebrated our wedding. Life was good, and we were satisfied; we had good jobs and good salaries. Periodically we heard from our loved ones in Mostar and sometimes we could send them some money . . . Again, everything was under my control, and once again I forgot God, prayer, and my promises to Him.

A few months after our wedding, the firm where I worked when I first arrived in Cyprus and through which I had my visa shut down, leaving me without a work visa. I needed to leave the country for a time to apply for a work visa at another job. Since the war in former Yugoslavia was coming to an end, the easiest and cheapest thing for me to do was to go to my family in Belgrade. The situation had calmed down: there was no longer a draft, nor the threat of airstrikes, the economic sanctions were lifted, and planes were flying again. I traveled to Belgrade, and Sanja stayed in Cyprus.

In the Second World War, the whole of my father's family escaped from Mostar to Belgrade. When the war was over, only my grandma and father returned to Mostar, leaving a lot of family on my father's side in Belgrade. The cousin with whom we lived in Cyprus expanded his business and offered me a job working for him. Another of my father's cousins and her husband suggested that Sanja and I care for them as they got older, and in return we would inherit their considerable property. In Cyprus, there were some complications with my work application, so Sanja and I agreed that she would join me in Belgrade. The property we were to inherit was large, and the job offer wasn't bad either. Sanja came, we rented a small apartment, and very soon after her arrival she got pregnant. The situation in Mostar was calm, so we could communicate with our loved ones more regularly. I was satisfied with my job, Sanja got hired in an exclusive boutique, and family took care of us . . . and again God had no place in my life.

Toward the end of Sanja's pregnancy, my mother came to visit us from Mostar. We hadn't seen each other for three years. She was one of the first people to travel to Serbia with a Croatian passport; she had to travel the long way through Hungary. A trip that would normally take six to seven hours, took a day and a half. When she arrived, I realized there was something different about my dear old mother. In addition to talking a lot about God and Jesus, she radiated a supernatural peace and joy. She brought us a Bible as a gift and talked about how God had changed her life. The visit was short and soon she returned to Mostar. The peace she had, and the change we saw in her, left a deep impression upon us.

The pregnancy went along normally, although the doctors suggested Sanja have a Caesarian section, due to problems she had with her spine as a child. As a developing teenager, she wore a medical brace for her spine, so there was a risk that her hips wouldn't open enough during labor, a danger for both her and the baby. In August 1995, Jovana was born by Caesarean section, 8 lbs., 4 oz. and 16.5 inches. Immediately following birth, the doctor sensed something wasn't okay with her, and referred us to go directly from the maternity ward to a specialist for diseases of the central nervous system. Dr. Radovanović was one of the best doctors in the region, an eminent expert with a lot of experience. After examining Jovana, she called us to her office and informed us that, even though she did not have all the necessary test results, Jovana was clearly a child with special needs who would have problems in development and wouldn't be able to walk. She sent us for an EEG, an ultrasound of the brain, a blood test, and some other tests, and asked that we return with all the results to get a final diagnosis and speak about possible treatments.

Sanja and I were heart-broken. We went home and I closed myself off in a room. After a long time, I was on my knees again in prayer. The prayer was different this time. Previously, I would plead with God, state my needs, expectations, and requests, and then, at the end, promise Him something in return (i.e., I will stop smoking or swearing, or I will do some good deed). I thought it was the same with God as with people, if you do me a favor I need to return it. But this time was different . . . I started to pray and at once I felt like God was talking to me. It wasn't a voice I could hear, but more like a thought popped into my head. I didn't like what I heard. God told me I was a hypocrite and that I sought Him only when I needed Him, and that I made promises to Him that I never kept . . . I felt bad, dirty, and sinful.

The next day I got in contact with my mom and shared the sad news with her, and asked her to pray for Jovana. She said she would pray as well as her church. I prayed every day. We did all the necessary tests, and I especially remember the electroencephalogram (EEG). We had to put Jovana to sleep, and they attached various wires to her head. Sanja held her in her arms, and I wiped the tears from Sanja's cheeks, so they wouldn't fall on Jovana and wake her up. When we gathered all the results, we went again to see Dr. Radovanović. She examined Jovana with a serious expression, read the test results, and then called us into her office. After we entered and sat down she said, "I don't know how to tell you this . . . " Sanja started to cry, and I thought the worse. The doctor got up and told Sanja not to cry, she had good news—her initial diagnosis was wrong. She said she had years of experience and had been known to make mistakes in the past, but she had never made such a big mistake. Jovana was completely healthy, and she didn't know how she made such an error.

At that point, I jumped up and for the first time I admitted publicly that I had prayed, and that I believed God healed Jovana. The doctor answered that she was an atheist and that she didn't believe in God. Her diagnosis was wrong, but in any case, she was glad that Jovana was okay.

I believed that God healed Jovana, and I wanted to repay Him in some way. I started to read the Bible that my mother left me when she visited us. I tried to live in harmony with what I considered moral and what pleased God, but I was completely frustrated. I caught myself lying; no matter how hard I tried to quit swearing I failed; I was envious; I was jealous . . . I even stopped smoking, but after a month and a half, I started again. It looked like God's standards were too high, and I couldn't fulfill them. I was right.

Many years later I heard a good definition from my friend, Michael Green, of what I tried to achieve. He said, "The religions of the world are rather like a ladder by which we try to reach up to God. But unfortunately, the ladder does not reach, for two reasons. God is infinite and we are mere mortals, and God is perfect and we are not. So inevitably religion is not going to reach God. We may climb up a few rungs of the ladder but then we fall off or find that the rungs are rotten and will not bear our weight. The unique thing about Jesus is that He came down to our world, kicked aside the ladder of religion, and offers fellowship with all who want it. Jesus offers us not religion, but relationship."

The first Sunday of my mom's visit, while Sanja was still pregnant with Jovana, she asked me to take her to the Evangelical church that was right in the center of town, just below Republic Square, which she heard about from her pastor in Mostar. I objected and said that she was silly, that she hadn't seen her son for three years and didn't need to waste her time in church, that the world wouldn't end if she missed a Sunday . . . Nothing worked, she was persistent and insisted that I drive her. That Sunday when we got to the church, I was stubborn and didn't want to go in with her, telling her I would wait in the hallway. They had installed speakers through which you could hear the service, so I heard my first sermon sitting in the hallway, in rebellion, waiting for my mom. After Jovana's healing, I decided to start going to that church.

Through listening to sermons, reading the Bible, and talking with friends I met in church, I started to understand that it wasn't about what I could do for God, but about what He did for me on the cross about two thousand years ago. I started to understand that God's standards are too high and that there was no way I could fulfill them in my own power and strength. At the same time, I started to realize that Jesus died on the cross and gave His life so that His life could pay the penalty for my sin. It didn't make sense to me how someone who lived two millenia before me could pay the penalty for my sins and why someone who didn't know me personally would want to do that. It seemed unfair to me that someone who didn't mess up should be punished in the place of someone who did. How can God, if He is righteous and holy, allow this? I was stuck and I didn't know how to go forward.

11.

The True Cross

Crux Sola Est Nostra Theologia

"The cross alone is our theology."

—MARTIN LUTHER

THE PROCESSION NEARED THE end of its mile-and-a-half walk from the Scuola Grande di San Giovanni Evangelista to the church of San Lorenzo in Venice. The streets along the canal were packed with Venetian citizens and visiting dignitaries. The members of the Scuola, dressed in full length white robes and clerical hats, led the procession over the arched stone bridge of San Lorenzo within sight of the church. At the heart of the crowd, beneath a canopy held aloft by four members of the confraternity, was the reason for the procession—an elaborate golden reliquary, ornately formed in the shape of a cross, holding a fragment from the cross on which Christ died. As the True Cross (as it was called) reached the crest of the bridge, the throng surged with excitement, jostling the cross-bearer. In a moment of confusion and panic, he lost hold of the relic and it fell over the parapet into the canal below.

A wave of alarm washed over the people. Some men threw themselves into the murky waters to rescue the cross before it was pulled to the bottom by the weight of its precious ornamentation. However, to everyone's shock, the cross did not sink. In fact, it did not even touch the water. The True Cross hovered above the canal sustained by the invisible power of the divine. Equally miraculous, the cross evaded attempts at rescue. The men who swam to it or approached it in a gondola were unable to grasp the True

Cross. Only when the Grand Guardian of the Scuola jumped into the canal did the cross gracefully move his way and allow itself to be returned to the procession. At least this is the story told more than a century later, in 1500, by Gentile Bellini in his painting *Miracle of the Cross at the Bridge of San Lorenzo* which hung in the Scuola Grande di San Giovanni Evangelista.

Relics were an important part of medieval Europe. Churches and monasteries with well-known relics drew pilgrims from across the region. Miraculous stories circulated about these relics only adding to their popularity. But no other relic could compare with the True Cross. To have a piece of the cross on which Christ died was to have something of value.

The origin of the True Cross goes back a thousand years from the Miracle of San Lorenzo. In 327, Emperor Constantine sent his mother Helena to Palestine to bring back relics from the life of Jesus, particularly to search for the cross. After consulting with locals in Jerusalem, she determined that the location of Jesus' death, burial, and resurrection was beneath the Temple of Venus built by Hadrian. Helena had the temple destroyed and the site excavated. While uncovering Jesus' tomb they discovered three crosses buried together. According to some later reports, one of the crosses was buried with a *titulus* matching the one nailed above Jesus' head in the biblical account. Helena was confident that she had found the True Cross but could not be sure which was the cross of Christ and which were the crosses of the thieves crucified on his right and left. Marcarius, the leader of the city, had a solution for the Empress. The three crosses were taken to the home of a woman on her deathbed. When the dying woman touched the first two crosses, nothing happened. However, when she touched the third cross, she sat up, completely well. This was all the confirmation Helena needed.

When Helena left Jerusalem to return to Rome, she left a section of the cross in the care of the bishop of Jerusalem encased in a silver reliquary. She took the remaining portion with her to Rome to keep in her private chapel. She also took back the three nails which affixed Christ to the cross. One of the nails she attached to Constantine's helmet for protection and another she had integrated into his bridle.

A nun named Egeria went on pilgrimage to Jerusalem about a half century after Helena's discovery. She wrote back to the sisters in her convent describing the veneration of the True Cross: "A silver-gilt casket is brought in which is the holy wood of the Cross. The casket is opened and [the wood] is taken out, and both the wood of the Cross and the title are placed upon the table. Now, when it has been put upon the table, the bishop, as he sits, holds the extremities of the sacred wood firmly in his hands, while the deacons who stand around guard it. It is guarded thus because the custom is that the people, both faithful and catechumens, come one by one and, bowing down at the table, kiss the sacred wood and pass through. And because, I know not when, someone is said to have bitten off and stolen a portion of the sacred wood, it is thus guarded by the deacons who stand around, lest anyone approaching should venture to do so again. And as all the people pass by one by one, all bowing themselves, they touch the Cross and the title, first with their foreheads and then with their eyes; then they kiss the Cross and pass through, but none lays his hand upon it to touch it."

By the 14th and 15th century, pieces of the True Cross were in churches across Europe. But it wasn't just the cross that was venerated. The bones of saints lay under altars, their teeth, hair, and fingers encased in gold and jewels. Relic collectors claimed to have the cup Jesus used at the last supper and clippings of his beard. Others claimed to possess the veil of Mary and some of her breast milk. Even more fantastically, others claimed to have a vial containing the breath of an angel. The faithful of Europe would travel hundreds of miles to experience the miraculous power of these relics, bringing with them prosperity and renown for the owners. The marketplace of relics became so widespread that both salesmen and consumers went to great lengths to obtain them.

People were wary of buying relics because they doubted anyone would sell an authentic one. This meant the best way to obtain a relic was to either steal it or buy a stolen one. According to their reasoning, it was not immoral to steal a relic because if the relic did not want to be stolen, it would make itself impossible to lift. However, if a saint allowed his bones to be stolen, then he must want to move because of something the current location did or didn't do.

So, you can imagine the joy of the Scuola in Venice when they received a piece of the True Cross. The prestige associated with the relic and the miracles attributed to it transformed a small lay community into a powerful and influential association in Venice.

During this period, certain leaders within the church began to speak against the relic market and the superstition they saw associated with it. Although these men came from different backgrounds and highlighted different errors within the church, one thing united them—they saw Jesus' death on the cross as the key factor for a relationship with God.

John Wycliffe, who lived in England during the 14th century, spoke out against the corrupting influence of power and money in the church. He created two translations of the Bible, encouraging people to connect with God through His Word rather than solely through the religious exercises of the church. He accused church leaders of using superstition to fill their coffers and maintain control over the people. "These wicked prelates sell Christian men's souls to Satan for money, for which souls Christ shed his precious heart's-blood upon the cross."

Wycliffe's writings influenced a church leader in Prague named Jan Hus. Like Wycliffe, he opposed the abuse of power by members of the church and appealed directly to Jesus and the Word of God for his final authority. Unlike Wycliffe, he was not allowed to live out his life. Hus was put on trial by the Church and condemned on July 6, 1415 for teaching heresy. He refused to recant his teachings unless shown from the Bible where he had erred. So condemned, he was led out into a courtyard, tied to a post, and burned to death. While Hus' life could be extinguished, the movement he was a part of could not.

A century passed before a German priest nailed 95 Theses against the Church to the doors of Wittenberg Chapel. Martin Luther, like Wycliffe and Hus before him, opposed those things in the church that distracted from the truth of God's Word. He wrote that "relics like the nails and the wood of the cross—they are the greatest lies." Luther loved the cross. One of his rallying cries was Crux Sola Est Nostra Theologica which means "the cross alone is our theology." However, when Luther spoke of the true cross, he was not referring to the wood found buried in Jerusalem, but to the supernatural work Jesus did in Jerusalem.

According to Luther, the faithful did not need to travel hundreds of miles in search of absolution, nor did they need to purchase forgiveness from the Church. They could go directly to the cross where Jesus died and find cleansing for their sins. Luther, like Hus, was put on trial. He also refused to recant "unless I am convinced by the testimony of the Holy Scriptures." He, too, was condemned a heretic in 1521. However, Luther was able to escape capture and live another 25 years writing, teaching, and establishing the new reformation movement.

When Luther died in 1546, John Calvin had already been continuing his reforming work for a decade in France and Switzerland. Calvin believed the church, with its relics and ceremonies, had distracted people from the message of the Bible. Regarding the True Cross he wrote, "Now let us consider how many relics of the true cross there are in the world. An account of those merely with which I am acquainted would fill a whole volume, for there is not a church, from a cathedral to the most miserable abbey or parish church, that does not contain a piece . . . In short, if we were to collect all these pieces of the true cross exhibited in various parts, they would form a whole ship's cargo." Calvin wanted to turn people's attention from relics like the True Cross to simple worship in God. He went so far as to remove all physical symbols out of the church, including crosses. For Calvin, the miraculous power of God was not in an object, but in Jesus who died on the cross and rose again three days later. The church walls were bear in the hope that the believers' hearts would be full. "If believers' eyes are turned to the power of the resurrection, in their hearts the cross of Christ will at last triumph over the devil, flesh, sin, and wicked men."

So, what about the miraculous cross of the Scuola Grande in Venice? When miraculous power resides in an object, like a relic or the True Cross, then that power is controlled by the owner of the object. But when the miraculous belongs to God alone, the One who can work whenever and however He wants, then the power is accessible to all men whatever their station in life. There is no need for the pageantry of a procession. Through prayer, the miraculous is always near. So, what is the true cross? Is it a splinter of wood drawn from the dirt three centuries after Jesus' death and encased in gold and silver? Or is it the historical event in which the perfect Son of God gave His life for His rebellious creation? As Calvin wrote, "For in the cross of Christ, as in a splendid theatre, the incomparable goodness of God is set before the whole world."

12.

Life or Death?

"God proved His love on the Cross. When Christ hung, and bled, and died, it was God saying to the world, 'I love you.'"

—BILLY GRAHAM

AN OLD BOSNIAN JOKE says that someone rang Mujo's door and when Mujo opened it he found a masked man with a pistol in his hand. The man said to him, "Your money, or your life." In response, Mujo called to his wife Fata and said, "Fata, my life, someone is asking for you."

Jokes always make us laugh, that is their purpose, but what is our life really? What do we mean by that word—life? Life is a biological term that speaks about the whole spectrum of processes in every living being, but the word "life" is also a philosophical term and many philosophers try to comprehend the meaning of life. What is life for you?

Proverbs 4:23 says, "Keep your heart with all vigilance, for from it flow the springs of life." Is the heart that beats and the blood that flows in our veins all that makes up life? Is this what Proverbs is saying or was wise Solomon thinking about something else besides the physical heart? Is life something more than this? Is life just food on the table, a fast and modern car, a new smartphone, and a full wallet? Is life just good health, good friends, the love of a boyfriend or girlfriend, or a happy marriage? John Lennon said, "Life is what happens to you while you are busy making other plans." We all make plans for life, and we want to live out our biological lives in good health and strength, but from the philosophical side, we also want our lives to have meaning, we want our lives to be fulfilling and purposeful. But what connection does the cross have with life?

In the Gospel of John chapter 10, Jesus compares Himself to a shepherd and believers to sheep. This is not an uncommon picture in the Bible; it often uses the picture of a shepherd for God, a flock of sheep for God's people, and a sheep/lamb for an individual believer. Even the great King David was a shepherd in his youth. One of the best-known places in the Bible is the oft-read and frequently quoted 23rd Psalm:

> "The LORD is my shepherd; I shall not want.
> He makes me lie down in green pastures. He leads me beside still waters.
> He restores my soul. He leads me in paths of righteousness for his name's sake.
> Even though I walk through the valley of the shadow of death, I will fear no evil, for you are with me; your rod and your staff, they comfort me.
> You prepare a table before me in the presence of my enemies; you anoint my head with oil; my cup overflows.
> Surely goodness and mercy shall follow me all the days of my life, and I shall dwell in the house of the LORD forever."

The psalmist of Psalm 23, King David, writes that God cares for him so he lacks nothing, that He gives him rest, direction for life, protection, and provision for his material, spiritual, and emotional needs. Jesus says about Himself in John 10 that He is the Good Shepherd who cares for His sheep, and that He knows them—every one of them—by name and that the sheep know Him. Also in that chapter, Jesus talks about the enemy of the sheep, about a thief that comes to steal, kill, and destroy, about a wolf that snatches and scatters the sheep. Jesus says about Himself, "I came that they may have life and have it abundantly."[1] And then He adds, "I am the good shepherd. The good shepherd lays down his life for the sheep."[2]

Jesus uses the picture of a shepherd prepared to give his life for the sheep, so that the sheep can have an abundant life. The sheep are a picture of me and you! Jesus was willing to give His life that we could live an abundant life! Jesus was not only willing to give His life, He did it willingly as he says in verse 17, "For this reason the Father loves me, because I lay down my life that I may take it up again . . . " Here Jesus is speaking about his

1. John 10:10b
2. John 10:11

death on the cross and resurrection. But which life does Jesus have in mind, the biological, or the philosophical, or both, or some third definition of life?

The word "life" is mentioned more than 400 times in the Bible—most of the books of the Bible include it—appearing for the first time at the very beginning, in the first chapter of the Bible in Genesis 1, and for the last time in the last chapter of the Bible, Revelation 22. From this we can conclude that life is a very important biblical concept. According to Bible dictionaries, the word "life" is not used in the Bible only to represent general life, physical and biological, but also figurative life—for immortality, for the way we spend life, for spiritual life and salvation, and for God and Jesus as the absolute source and cause of all life.

When Jesus says He gives His life so the sheep can have life, He is thinking about all the above. He isn't just talking about life after death, nor only about the life we now live. He came to remove the burden of sin, to redeem us, to pay the penalty for our sins with His life, and to remove the barrier of sin that stands between us and God. He gave His life on the cross, not just that we would have eternal life, but that we could live this life now fully and, as Jesus Himself said, abundantly. Jesus is not talking about material abundance (even though it's not necessarily excluded), he is talking about abundance of spirit and soul!

When I think of Jesus and His parable of the good shepherd and the sheep, I remember the stories my good Macedonian friend, Kosta, told me. His grandpa was a shepherd and he had a large flock of sheep. As a high school student, Kosta would go to his grandma and grandpa's during school breaks. One day his grandpa asked him to take the sheep out to pasture. Many times, he had watched how his grandpa led the sheep, and it looked easy: Grandpa would move and the sheep would follow, then Grandpa would stop to talk to a friend leaning on his shepherd's staff, and all the sheep would stop and wait for him to move. As he went, if any sheep lagged behind, he would call it, and it would run to him. Kosta thought it would be an easy task. He started out, and the sheep went the other direction, he ran after them, and they ran from him, he didn't know them, nor did they know him. He came home frustrated and without half the flock. But Jesus says, "I am the good shepherd. I know my own and my own know me."[3] And, "My sheep hear my voice, and I know them, and they follow me. I give them eternal life, and they will never perish, and no one will snatch them

3. John 10:14

out of my hand."[4] What a wonderful picture of God and His people—the good shepherd who cares for His flock, the shepherd who was willing to give His life that the sheep could have a full life. He died so the sheep could live. At the end of the chapter, we see the Jews who were listening to Him had no doubts that He was calling Himself God. It was so clear to them that they wanted to stone Him for blasphemy, but, as we read in the Bible, Jesus escaped from their grasp.

After the parable of the shepherd and the sheep, we read in the eleventh chapter about some of Jesus' friends. At the beginning of the chapter, we meet Lazarus and his sisters Mary and Martha from Bethany and find out that Jesus loved them. We learn that Lazarus is sick, very sick, and that Mary and Martha have sent a messenger to Jesus. After the messenger arrives and gives Him the news, Jesus doesn't go immediately, but sets off two days later despite the opposition of the disciples who remember the recent stoning attempt. Jesus and His disciples arrive in Bethany to discover that Lazarus is dead and has been buried for four days. Dead, buried, and in his grave for four days. At the high temperatures common in Israel, the body has already started to decay and stink after four days. It is too late to do anything. That's what Lazarus' sister, Martha, thinks when she hears that Jesus is coming and runs out to meet Him. She is disappointed that Jesus hasn't come sooner because she believes that Jesus could have healed him like He healed many sick people while He announced the arrival of God's Kingdom. "Jesus said to her, 'I am the resurrection and the life. Whoever believes in me, though he die, yet shall he live, and everyone who lives and believes in me shall never die.'"[5]

If Jesus had stopped there with that statement, we could think that He was overstating things, or that He didn't literally mean what He said. But after this statement, Jesus did something incredible, something unfathomable, something an ordinary man couldn't do. What did Jesus do? After Martha left and called her sister Mary, they returned to Jesus, along with the Jews that were in their house. They went to express their condolences and grieve for Lazarus. Jesus asked to see where Lazarus was buried. The Bible tells us that Jesus, seeing Mary and Martha and their friends crying, began to weep. When they arrived at the grave, Jesus commanded for it to be opened, to which Martha replied that Lazarus had already been dead for four days and would smell, stink. When they opened the grave,

4. John 10:27–28
5. John 11:25–26

Jesus prayed and called out in a loud voice, "Lazarus, come out!" Lazarus come out? He said this to a man who was already dead for four days and whose body had already started to decay? And He did it in front of all those people? What happened? The deceased came out. The deceased came out! Man cannot bring man back to life, only God can do that!

Skeptics may say Lazarus only experienced a clinical death. We have all heard cases of people experiencing a clinical death only to wake up after some time on an operating table or after a few hours in the morgue. But after four days, after the body had started to decay and stink? Three to four hours after death, rigor mortis sets in—the convulsion of the muscles that lasts 36–48 hours after which the body starts to decay. Lazarus' body had started to rot and decay; that wasn't clinical death, that was a miracle. God Himself performed this miracle to confirm His incredible statement, "I am the resurrection and the life. Whoever believes in me, though he die, yet shall he live, and everyone who lives and believes in me shall never die."[6]

After this kind of miracle who could oppose Jesus' statement? Returning to Jesus' tears, if He knew Lazarus would rise from the dead why did He cry? I believe He cried because of the people's unbelief. God, the one who could perform miracles, stood among them and they neither believed, nor sought, nor expected anything from Him. The solution to the problem was there, before them, within their grasp, but they didn't recognize Him.

Later in the Bible we read that many of those present that day, having seen what Jesus did, believed in Him. We also see that some went and told the religious leaders all that had happened. The chief priests felt threatened. They felt Jesus was calling them out even more than He did when He healed the man blind from birth,[7] and more than He did in the parable of the good shepherd[8] where He clearly called them out for not caring correctly for God's "flock." And now He dared to raise a man from the dead! They decided to kill Him. They still didn't know how they would do it. They still didn't know that it would happen on their great holiday—Passover. They still didn't know that Jesus would die a martyr's death on a cross and that through this death on a cross He would fulfill the purpose for which He had come into the world. Maybe it seems strange that not everyone present believed, that the chief priests were so opposed they decided to kill Jesus,

6. John 11:25–26
7. John 9
8. John 10

but the Bible says that "the word of the cross is folly to those who are perishing, but to us who are being saved it is the power of God."[9]

Lazarus continued his life. In the twelfth chapter we see that a few days before Jesus' death and resurrection, He visited Bethany again and had dinner with Martha, Mary, and Lazarus and that Lazarus sat with Him at the table. We also read that the religious leaders decided to kill Lazarus because he was a living, walking, and breathing witness to Jesus' divinity. We don't know if this happened or how and when Lazarus finished his life, but we know for sure at some point Lazarus died again. Did Jesus' statement, "Whoever believes in me, though he die, yet shall he live," cease to be valid then, or did Lazarus go from death into eternal life?

A couple of years ago, at a time when I had some major problems, I received an email with an inspirational message from Ben, a friend in Holland. The message said, "If the devil knocks on your door, send Jesus to answer it." I was reminded that Jesus gave His life on the cross so I could have eternal life, and not only that, but this life I now live I can live abundantly with God's blessing, protection, care—a life in which He cares for my needs, spiritual, emotional, physical . . . like King David so eloquently wrote in Psalm 23. Now the choice is up to me. When the thief knocked on Mujo's door and asked for his money or his life, Mujo sent Fata. When the devil knocks on my door and asks for my life, will I open it or send Jesus?

9. 1 Corinthians 1:18

13.

Homecoming

"I think that whatever you look for in God you'll still have to pass through that door of humility and that door of complete vulnerability that a child has."

—BONO VOX

THE WAR IN BOSNIA and Herzegovina was over, Sanja and I were working, Jovana grew and thrived, and we could communicate more regularly with our families in Mostar. We were going to a friend's place in Montenegro on the sea and afterwards to the mountains to my aunt's weekend house in Zlatibor, Serbia . . . life was good again. We even organized a meeting with Sanja's parents, my mother, and my sister with her family in Berkovići, a village near Mostar on the demarcation line. A single phone call changed this idyll. I was informed that my mother was really sick, and the diagnosis was leukemia. She was urgently transported to Zagreb for treatment. After a couple of weeks, they returned her to Mostar. My sister told me the prognosis was not very good, and I should come and visit Mom.

There were two problems: first, Sanja and I swore we would never return to BiH, and secondly, I was afraid to cross the war line of demarcation because the bloodshed and war had just recently ended. In spite of this, I decided to take the trip. Five years had passed since I left Mostar and Herzegovina. Even though it was not necessary to travel through Hungary anymore, there still wasn't a direct line. From Belgrade, I could go by bus to Srpsko Sarajevo (the Serb part of Sarajevo), cross over the line of demarcation on foot, take a taxi to the bus station in Sarajevo and then a bus to Mostar.

I started out with a friend whose family we met in Cyprus, and with whom we continued to socialize when they returned from Cyprus to Serbia. She had a sister in Sarajevo that she had already visited. We decided not to take the bus to Srpsko Sarajevo, but instead we got out in Pale, took a "Serbian" taxi to the demarcation line, and then switched to a "Bosnian" taxi that took us to the center of Sarajevo. At the demarcation line, next to the tunnel exit, there was a cafe with a symbolic name, Dayton, named after the city in the US where the peace accord was signed. Taxi drivers from both sides came to the cafe to "transfer" passengers. In the taxi, I learned it was best to keep my mouth shut. In answer to the driver's question as to where we were traveling and my answer that I am going to Mostar, we started to comment on the situation in Mostar. The second part of the war in Mostar was between Croats and Bosniaks.

Since after the war Sarajevo was for the most part a Bosnian city, I had assumed that the driver was Bosniak. Because he knew we came from the Republika Srpska (Serb Republic), I wanted to gain his favor a little, so I started to blame the Croats for the events in Mostar. After my monologue, he told me things weren't always as they seemed, and that he was Croat. Today, I still don't know if he was honest with me, or if he just wanted to joke with me, but in that taxi, I learned an important life lesson.

We got out of the taxi at the Sarajevo Cathedral; my friend, Silvana, went to her sister's, and I started out toward the bus station. I remember being overwhelmed by emotions seeing the destroyed and damaged buildings, especially the "Sarajevo Roses"—mortar holes around the city filled in with red resin as a memorial to those who died in the explosion. The bus trip to Mostar wasn't any easier—scene after scene of demolished and burned villages and destroyed and robbed houses . . . human casualties were not visible, but I knew many had lost their lives.

My arrival in Mostar was a great shock. In my five-year absence, things had changed drastically; a picture of destruction and war on every corner. In the air there was tension and in conversation with people there was a feeling of inter-ethnic bigotry, blaming "them" for all that had happened. In my sister's apartment, there was an eruption of emotion . . . my sister, my brother-in-law, their three children, the youngest born during the war who I met only briefly in Berkovići, and my mother bedridden with a surgical mask on her face to protect her from infections that could destroy her already weakened body. But, surrounding my mother there was a strange peace. Instead of encouraging and comforting her, she encouraged and comforted us.

One afternoon, friends from church let us know they were coming to visit her. A few of them came, and we had a casual, relaxing conversation. Then they wanted to pray for my mother. After praying for my mom, one woman, who I later found out was named Ivon, Pastor Karmelo's wife, asked if she could pray for me. I consented. She started to pray, and though I don't remember the words of the prayer, I do remember that all at once I was overcome with emotion. Tears filled my eyes and rolled down my face; an unexplainable joy filled my heart, so that I laughed and cried at the same time. When Ivon finished her prayer, I felt a little strange and ashamed because I thought that my behavior—tears and laughter—would disgrace my mother, but she didn't seem to mind.

In the Evangelical Church of Mostar, where my mom was a member, some guests came from abroad to host a series of sermons and lectures. Mom, though weak, sick, bald, and wearing a surgical mask, wanted to go to the church for one of the talks and insisted I go with her. When we arrived, the church was already full of people. The program started, first a few songs and then the teaching. The preacher told an Old Testament story from the book of Daniel, the third chapter, about three young men who, because of their faith in God, were willing to risk being thrown alive into a fiery furnace, and who God delivered from the furnace in a miraculous way. I didn't understand everything—their names were especially unusual and strange.

After the sermon, someone spoke about Jesus. He said everything I already knew intellectually: that we are sinful people, and that Jesus—God—came in the flesh, was born as a man so He could become like us in every way except in regards to sin. He never sinned. He died an agonizing death on a cross to pay the penalty for our sins, for all of us, including me! Jesus died so I could have access to a holy, righteous, all-powerful God who doesn't tolerate sin. He paid the price—a high price—His life!

Intellectually I already knew all of this in my head, but I wasn't ready to accept it in my heart. The preacher said we needed to accept Jesus as our Lord and Savior. It wasn't clear to me what he meant by that, but he explained it. Jesus came to save us from the consequences of our sins, but if we wanted to receive this salvation then we had to accept Him as the Lord of our lives. God is not satisfied with second place in our lives—He can be either on the throne of our lives or not part of our lives.

The preacher nicely explained all this and gave an invitation. He said, "If there is anyone in this room who wants to receive Jesus and repent for his sins, let him come forward." I knew that I needed a Savior, and I wanted to go forward, but I wasn't ready. I looked around the church and saw some familiar faces, neighbors, and I asked myself what would they think about me. I stayed bolted to my chair.

After the program, Mom and I went to her apartment. After five years, I would again sleep in my childhood room. It was the same one in which, some years later, I would look through the window and see the construction of the cross on Hum. Because the apartment was quite close to the front line during the war, it was significantly damaged. On the front door, right above the peephole, there was a bullet hole, and in my mom's room the walls were damaged from a flurry of bullets. She told me that one evening she went into her room to find lots of dust in the air and a bullet on her pillow that would have ended up in her head had she gone to sleep a little earlier that evening.

Mom went to her room, and I went to mine. I lay down in bed, but tossed and turned, sleep was evasive. I started to think about Jesus, and the limitless, unconditional love He showed me on the cross. He died for me before I was born. He did it to save me from sin, to save me for eternity, to solve my problem, the problem of sin, which I was hopeless to solve myself. I had rejected Him, rejected that incredible offer. I knelt beside my bed and I started to pray. I could almost literally feel the weight of sin on my shoulders. I started to cry, to sob. I asked Jesus to forgive me for running away from Him, for seeking Him only when I needed Him, and for not going forward that evening when the preacher gave the invitation. I told Him that I wanted Him to be my Lord and Savior, and that I surrendered my life into His hands.

At that moment, I felt that someone else was in the room with me, I felt that Jesus was there, and in my head I heard God's voice telling me, "Arise, My child." I continued crying, but my tears of grief turned to tears of joy. I could feel the burden on my shoulders was no longer there. I stood up and started to thank God. I told Him that the next day I would go with my mom to church and if the preacher gave another invitation, I would go forward publicly, in front of everyone, to accept Jesus and repent for my sins. I did just that. That evening I made the most important decision of my life, a decision I have never regretted. Some of the things I experienced that evening have never left me.

I experienced love, unconditional love. This isn't the love the world knows. The world tells me, "If you love me, I'll love you. Do this for me, and I will do it for you." Jesus says, "I love you no matter what. I love you even when you don't love Me and when you reject Me. I went to the cross for you even when you didn't know Me." I experienced the love of Jesus, the same Jesus I had for years cursed and rejected, and whose followers I mocked. And He loves me, regardless of it all.

I experienced forgiveness, unconditional forgiveness. The forgiveness of this world says, "I will forgive you until you do something else against me, then I will remember it." The forgiveness of this world says, "I will forgive you, but never forget." When God forgives, He doesn't mention it anymore. I knew that I was forgiven and that He would never mention it again.

I experienced peace, and not the peace the world gives, but God's supernatural peace. Jesus told His disciples in one of the Gospels "Peace I leave with you . . . Let not your hearts be troubled." The peace that Jesus offers isn't the peace that this world knows. From that evening, I made peace with God that helped me find peace with myself and with other people.

I experienced joy, not this world's joy, but supernatural joy. This world's joy is dependent on circumstances. While everything is under my control, while everything is how I want it to be, I will be happy and joyful. But what happens when problems come knocking on our door or sickness or poverty or persecution or misunderstanding? The joy God gives does not depend on circumstances, but is unconditional joy. When it was hard, when I was unjustly accused, when there was not enough money to pay the bills, and when my life was in danger . . . the joy of the Lord was my strength.

I would never go back to the old way of living. Never!

14.

The Pilgrims of the Cross

"Whoever, therefore, shall determine upon this holy pilgrimage . . . shall wear the sign of the cross of the Lord on his forehead or on his breast. When, indeed, he shall return from his journey, having fulfilled his vow, let him place the cross on his back between his shoulders. Thus shall ye, indeed, by this twofold action, fulfill the precept of the Lord, 'he that taketh not his cross, and followeth after me, is not worthy of me.'"

—POPE URBAN, COUNCIL OF CLAIRMONT, 27 NOVEMBER 1095

THE SUMMER OF 1096, Bohemond was camped on the coast of the sea of Salerno laying siege to the rebellious city. He was a seasoned warrior, second to none in the art of war. In his twenties, Bohemond fought alongside his father in the Balkans, defeating better equipped Byzantine forces. He was an intimidating figure. Although his given name was Mark, his father, after hearing the whimsical tale of the giant *Buamundus Gigas* at a banquet, thought the name Bohemond more fitting for his oversized son. He stood a foot and a half above the tallest man. His broad shoulders, deep chest, and powerful arms, tapered down to a narrow waist. He was neither thin nor overweight, but perfectly proportioned for battle. His skin was pale white like his Norse ancestors, although his face was flushed red. His yellowish hair was cut close to the ears and his face clean-shaven. His blue eyes radiated a high spirit, and he carried himself with confident dignity. To those in Byzantium he was a barbarian but a barbarian not to be crossed. At only forty years old, he had spent half his life at war.

News reached Bohemond that a host of warriors from throughout the empire were marching to Jerusalem in response to a call to arms from Pope Urban. The very streets where the Lord Jesus walked, it was reported, were overrun with pagan hordes. The Holy Sepulchre of the Lord was possessed by unclean nations and the holy places were treated with irreverence and ignominy. The Pope was calling the Franks, that race on whom "God has conferred remarkable glory in arms, great courage, bodily activity, and strength to humble the hairy scalps of those who resist," to pick up their swords and put their faith into action. When Bohemond heard this report, his heart stirred within him.

"What do these pilgrims carry with them?" Bohemond asked.

"Arms suitable for battle," came the answer.

"And what is their battle cry?"

"They cry out the truth in one voice, 'God wills it! God wills it! God wills it!'"

"And what sign do they carry? By what symbol are they set apart?"

"On the right shoulder they wear the stigma of the Lord's passion, the emblem of the soldiery of God, the cross of Christ."

Bohemond stood and called for his finest cloak. Before those assembled, he made a vow to complete this pilgrimage to Jerusalem and to take up his cross as a living sacrifice, holy and acceptable to God. He then ordered his cloak cut into pieces and made into crosses. Most of the knights engaged in the siege rallied to him. They too took up the cross. Then, leaving the past behind them, they set out for Jerusalem, pilgrims of the cross.

In the same year as Bohemond's birth, 1054, there was a cataclysmic division in the Christian Church, known today as the Great Schism. There had been growing resentment between the western, Latin church under the Pope in Rome and the eastern Orthodox church under the Patriarch in Constantinople. The seeds of this resentment were differences in theology, doctrine, language, politics, and geography. But these seeds flowered into division as Pope Leo IX tried to exert worldwide primacy over the Church and Patriarch Cerularius ordered the closure of Latin churches in Constantinople. The end result was an irreparable divide through the heart of the church.

Divisions were not limited to the eastern and western churches, however. The Western church itself was fractured. The Normans, who were conquering southern Italy, were at odds with the Emperor and the Popes who supported him. Not long after the Great Schism, Pope Nicholas II made an alliance with the Normans, bringing them into the church and garnering their support against political factions from within. However, the relationship between the Imperial court and the Papacy was strained. In 1080, Emperor Henry IV deposed and excommunicated Pope Gregory VII, installing his own "anti-Pope," Clement III, in Rome. Here was the Western Christian world at war with itself in a power struggle between Church and State. Did the Church serve at the generous bequest of the Emperor? Or did the Emperor rule under the authority of the Church? With one Pope in exile in France and another under the Emperor's thumb in Rome, with rival lords in constant war with one another throughout the Empire, with Normans pressing from the south and the west, what was to become of the western Church? It was into this reality that Pope Urban II, in 1095, delivered what is perhaps the most influential speech in the history of Europe.

In March 1095, an envoy from Byzantine Emperor Alexius I came to the Council of Piacenza to request help against the Seljuq Turks who were steadily taking territory across Asia Minor. The envoy came with stories of churches desecrated and transformed into mosques, of pilgrims harassed and killed, of Christian villages depopulated by means of the sword and by fire. Alexius hoped for a small cohort of mercenaries to fight alongside his regular forces to stop the Seljuq encroachment. Instead, his request precipitated something altogether unexpected.

It was at the end of the year, November 27, in the French town of Clermont, that Pope Urban answered Alexius' call. During the final days of the Council, Urban addressed a large audience of French nobles and clergy. Added to this number, hundreds gathered in the field outside the city to hear him speak. Standing on the dais before the people he declared:

> *Your brethren who live in the east are in urgent need of your help, and you must hasten to give them the aid.*

In order to add motivation to the call, he demonized the enemy in the East.

> *. . . A race from the kingdom of the Persians, an accursed race, a race wholly alienated from God, a generation that set not their heart aright and whose spirit was not steadfast with God, violently invaded the lands of those Christians and has depopulated them by pillage and fire.*

Then, appealing to their brotherly sensibilities, he called them to remove their sword from the necks of their Christian brothers and point it at a common enemy.

> Let those who have been accustomed unjustly to wage private warfare against the faithful now go against the infidels and end with victory this war which should have been begun long ago. Let those who for a long time, have been robbers, now become knights. Let those who have been fighting against their brothers and relatives now fight in a proper way against the barbarians. Let those who have been serving as mercenaries for small pay now obtain the eternal reward. Let those who have been wearing themselves out in both body and soul now work for a double honor.

It was at this point that Urban made a choice that caused his words to echo across Europe and through the following generations. He did not set his sights on Constantinople and the Seljuq forces on its doorstep, but beyond. He looked to the Holy Land, to Jerusalem, to the location of the Sermon on the Mount and the cross and the resurrection.

> Enter upon the road to the Holy Sepulcher, wrest that land from the wicked race, and subject it to yourselves. Jerusalem is the center of the earth; the land is fruitful above all others, like another paradise of delights. This spot the Redeemer of mankind has made illustrious by his advent, has beautified by his sojourn, has consecrated by his passion, has redeemed by his death, has glorified by his burial. This royal city, however, situated at the center of the earth, is now held captive by the enemies of Christ and is subjected, by those who do not know God, to the worship of the heathen. She seeks, therefore, and desires to be liberated and ceases not to implore you to come to her aid.

By placing the focus on Jerusalem, Urban transformed his speech from a call to war to a call to pilgrimage. In the tradition of the Church, pilgrimage was a part of the penitential system. By going on a devotional journey, especially one of such expense and complexity as walking in the footsteps of Jesus, the pilgrim could express repentance and experience the purging of sin. But Urban was not calling for a traditional pilgrimage. This was an armed pilgrimage with eternal rewards.

> Whoever wishes to save his soul should not hesitate humbly to take up the way of the Lord, and if he lacks sufficient money, divine mercy will give him enough. Brethren, we ought to endure much suffering

for the name of Christ—misery, poverty, nakedness, persecution,
want, illness, hunger, thirst, and other ills of this kind, just as the
Lord said to His disciples: "Ye must suffer much in My name," and
"Be not ashamed to confess Me before the faces of men; verily I will
give you mouth and wisdom," and finally, "Great is your reward in
Heaven."

How glorious must that heavenly reward have seemed to those warriors weighed down by a lifetime of sin? Not only could they win earthly
glory and reward by defeating the enemy, they could secure their eternal
destination.

Undertake this journey eagerly for the remission of your sins, with
the assurance of the reward of imperishable glory in the kingdom of
heaven . . . All who die by the way, whether by land or by sea, or in
battle against the pagans, shall have immediate remission of sins.

The response to Urban's call was unanimous. Those in attendance rose
up and began to chant what became the battle cry of the crusades, "God
wills it! God wills it! God wills it!" Traveling preachers and monks began
spreading Urban's message throughout the Latin world. The result was an
unexpected and unprecedented reaction.

One historian from Bohemond's company described the response:
"When now that time was at hand which the Lord Jesus daily points out to
His faithful, especially in the Gospel, saying, 'If any man would come after
me, let him deny himself and take up his cross and follow me,' a mighty
agitation was carried on throughout all the region of Gaul. Its tenor was
that if anyone desired to follow the Lord zealously, with a pure heart and
mind, and wished faithfully to bear the cross after Him, he would no longer
hesitate to take up the way to the Holy Sepulchre."

The First Crusade represents a transition in the symbolic meaning of
the cross. The cross and the sword were intertwined. Religious and military symbolism were blended. The power shifted from the emperor to the
church. This simple symbol, when combined with the elements of Urban's
speech, created a movement that propelled both the powerful and the poor
to risk their lives for a higher cause. But what would be the consequences of
using the cross in this way?

On April 9, 1097, Bohemond arrived in Constantinople. Alexius, who
had personally fought against Bohemond in the Balkans fifteen years earlier, was tense. Throughout the spring, troops continued to arrive, growing
to as many as 75,000. The numbers were far greater than Alexius expected.

The Byzantine emperor considered these Latins barbarians. Constantinople was the center of Christian civilization at that time. As the Latin warriors saw the walls surrounding the city—sixty feet tall, fifteen feet thick, and four miles long—perhaps they felt barbaric in comparison. With half a million citizens, Constantinople was ten times larger than the largest city in the west. It also boasted the unparalleled Basilica of St. Sophia and a treasure trove of relics. Yet, Bohemond and the other princes reached an agreement with the Emperor. To them, it was the Turks who were barbarians. There was Alexius in the middle, aligning himself with barbarians from the west to defeat the barbarians to the east.

The warrior pilgrims crossed into Asia Minor and captured the fortified city of Nicaea after a four-month siege. By the end of June 1097, they set out across the mainland of Asia Minor, repelling attacks by Seljuq forces and battling the elements along the way. Crossing this land was not a given. Many future crusades failed to accomplish the feat, but Bohemond and his fellow princes managed to reach the edge of Syria by October 1097. This they did without a clear military leader. The princes operated as an army council, making most decisions by committee. While this would be disastrous in most military situations, the crusaders were united in a common cause. This cause could best be expressed in the rallying cry used to strengthen the men's resolve: "Stand fast together, trusting in Christ and the victory of the Holy Cross. Today may we all gain much booty." Religious fervor and self-advancement were interwoven in such a way that former enemies marched and fought side-by-side. The princes had agreed to a principle of "right by conquest," the idea that a captured city belonged to the first claimant or occupier. Most, like Bohemond, hoped to carve out their own fiefdom in the Levant. But greed alone does not explain the phenomenon of this first Crusade. Many who took up the cross made substantial financial sacrifices to participate with no expectation of making it back. Robert of Normandy, who marched with Bohemond, pawned all of Normandy to his brother King William of England in order to go. Godfrey of Bouillon sold the county of Verdun to the king of France to raise funds. These men never expected to see their lands again.

In June 1099, the surviving warriors reached Jerusalem after a journey of nearly 2000 miles and three years. Upon seeing the holy city and the Church of the Holy Sepulchre built by Constantine in the fourth century, many of these hardened warriors wept openly. The pilgrims of the cross had at last reached the place of the cross. In less than a month, they took

Jerusalem and fulfilled Pope Urban's call. On July 15, 1099, the place where Jesus lived and taught, was crucified and resurrected, was in Christian hands. A few weeks later, the Latin victors revealed a symbol of the success of the crusading ideal. It was called the True Cross. This relic, which was hidden by native Christians in Jerusalem during Muslim rule, was a battered silver and gold crucifix that contained a chunk of wood from the actual cross on which Jesus died. These men who had risked their lives to take up the cross as warrior pilgrims, could look upon the True Cross as a sign of their victory.

Bohemond, who had led the capture of Antioch and claimed the city for his own, remained in the Levant attempting to carve out the great eastern principality he desired. He faced opposition from Alexius' Byzantine Empire, as well as the Seljuq Turks he had displaced. By 1104, he was badly in need of reinforcements and returned to Europe in search of support. He was welcomed as a hero. Audiences across France were enchanted by his stories of perilous battles with the eastern barbarians and by the relics he brought with him from the Holy Land. His new-found status won him the hand of Constance, the beautiful daughter of Philip I, the king of France. Within a few years, he had gathered an army of more than 30,000 men. However, instead of using the forces to strengthen and defend Antioch, he set out to attack Alexius. The result was a humiliating defeat and his subjugation as vassal of the Byzantine Emperor. Bohemond died not long afterwards, a broken man, never having returned to the east.

In 1187 the Muslim world united and regained control of Jerusalem under the leadership of Saladin. Not long afterwards, Pope Innocent III called for a new crusade (now called the Fourth Crusade) to approach the Holy Land by way of Egypt. Much had changed since Urban's speech. Crusading was an established political tool and the remission of sins through indulgences had become an integrated part of the process. While Innocent echoed some of Urban's arguments, his call was more administrative and organizational. However, the Fourth Crusade never reached Egypt. After sacking the Christian city of Zara (Zadar) on the Adriatic coast, a means of gaining support from the Venetians, the crusaders arrived at Constantinople. This time, they were not going to pass through the city, they were going to destroy it. From April 12–15, 1204, the crusader army looted, raped, and murdered their way through the greatest city in Europe. They even went so far as to desecrate the great church Hagia Sophia, smashing icons, destroying holy books, and drinking liberally of the consecrated wine. Constantinople and the Byzantine Empire never fully recovered. It was not the "barbarian" Turks who brought down Constantinople but the very crusades organized to defeat them. And as these pilgrims spread chaos and bloodshed through the greatest Christian city on earth, they did so under one unified symbol—the cross.

Can we agree that these actions do not represent the true meaning of the cross? For the Western Empire to send troops to support the Eastern Empire against an opposing force was not the problem. Throughout history nations have formed alliances to defeat enemies and take new land. The tragedy of the Crusades was the hijacking of the cross. With the cross entwined with the sword, with forgiveness embedded in warfare, with eternal blessings confused with earthly rewards, the cross and all it stands for was left bleeding on the battlefield. You cannot twist the meaning of the cross without twisting the meaning of the Bible. You cannot change the meaning of the symbol without perverting the words of the one who died upon it. The greatest desolation of the Crusades was the true meaning of the cross.

On the 800th anniversary of the sacking of Constantinople, Pope John Paul II released an apology. "Some memories are especially painful, and some events of the distant past have left deep wounds in the minds and hearts of people to this day. I am thinking of the disastrous sack of the imperial city of Constantinople, which was for so long the bastion of Christianity in the East. It is tragic that the assailants, who had set out to secure free access for Christians to the Holy Land, turned against their own brothers in the faith. The fact that they were Latin Christians fills Catholics with deep regret. How can we fail to see here the mystery of evil at work in the human heart?"

What happens when you invoke a symbol as powerful as the cross without regard to the "mystery of evil at work in the human heart?"—the Crusades. Can the true meaning of the cross be rescued from such history? And where does the cross belong? Does it belong on the broad shoulders of Bohemond? Or on the burning lawn of Martin Luther King, Jr.? Or on a hill above Sarajevo or Mostar? Or on the flag of Dunant? How can anyone hope to take up his cross and follow Jesus without knowing what that means?

15.

Burden or Calling?

"I didn't go to religion to make me 'happy.' I always knew a bottle of port would do that. If you want a religion to make you feel really comfortable, I certainly don't recommend Christianity."

—C.S. LEWIS

ARTHUR BLESSITT IS ONE of the few people in the world who can say, "I've been to your country," even before he asks where you are from. You see, Arthur Blessitt has walked through every sovereign nation and populated island in the world—324 countries to be exact. Arthur holds the Guinness World Record for the longest ongoing walk in history at 41,879 miles. That is more than one and half times the circumference of the earth. Most surprising of all, he did this while carrying a twelve foot, 45 pound wooden cross.

In 1969, Arthur Blessitt felt compelled by God to take the wooden cross down from the wall of his church on Sunset Strip in Los Angeles and carry it across America to Washington D.C. This initial journey then extended beyond his home country. By 2008, he had walked across all seven continents (including Antarctica), carried the cross to the top of Mount Kilamenjaro and along the Great Wall of China, traversed 54 war zones, interacted with world leaders, and met millions of diverse people. The cross itself was broken, stolen, cast overboard, and lost. Yet, each time it was repaired, rescued, and recovered. Arthur Blessitt, who at 76 years of age continues to add steps to his journey, still carries the cross he took down from the wall of his church half a century ago.

What possesses a man to carry a wooden cross around the globe?

The first mention of the cross in the Bible is found in the tenth chapter of Matthew's gospel. Jesus had already given His famous Sermon on the Mount and was, by this point, followed everywhere by large crowds. He had chosen twelve men to be His closest followers, His disciples, and He was preparing them to go out with His message, "Repent, for the kingdom of heaven is at hand." While he promised to give them power to succeed at the task, he warned them it will not be easy. Religious leaders and political agents would oppose them, arrest them, even beat them. But they were not to fear because that was what it means to be His followers. He said, "Do not think that I have come to bring peace to the earth, I have not come to bring peace, but a sword." These are surprising words from Jesus. Isn't Jesus all about peace and harmony? Why would He come with a sword? Jesus knew that His message was divisive. He knew that some of His followers would have to choose between family and faith. He knew that following Him only works as a priority in life. It could never be second.

To accentuate this point, Jesus said, "Whoever does not take his cross and follow me is not worthy of me." What did Jesus mean by this statement? Was He meaning we all should build giant crosses and follow Blessitt's example?

There is a part of Jesus' sermon that sounds more like a Crusader motto than words of Jesus. During the Crusades, the phrase "taking up the cross" or "bearing the cross" was synonymous with going on a crusade. To wear the red cross on your cloak also meant taking up your sword. But as we have seen in the last chapter, this is not the true meaning of the cross. So what did Jesus mean by telling His followers to take up their cross?

First of all, the image of Jesus on the cross would have been far from the disciples' minds. Not only had Jesus not yet been crucified, but the thought was unimaginable to the disciples at that time. However, they had all seen the crucifixion process. They had seen someone carrying the implement of his death to the location of his death. This would have been familiar to them. And this seems to be the point Jesus was making. After telling His disciples to take up their cross, He said, "Whoever finds his life will lose it, and whoever loses his life for my sake will find it."

The cross is clearly related to losing your life. Jesus was telling His disciples that if they were not willing to lose their lives for Him, then they were not worthy of being His followers. These are very strong words.

During Arthur Blessitt's first extended journey with the cross—from California to Washington D.C.—he faced some unexpected resistance. He and a friend were pulling the cross, which at that time weighed 110 pounds, alongside a road in Indiana when they were approached by three angry men. One of the men was carrying a gasoline can which he had just filled up at the station across the road. They shouted, "You better get out of the way because we are going to burn that cross, and you too if you try to stop us." Arthur's friend turned white. He didn't know what to do. Meanwhile Arthur, who was lost in thought and didn't hear the threat, turned to his friend and said, "Hey, why don't we get a coke, I'm thirsty." They turned and walked toward the gas station, the three men trailing behind in confusion. Arthur, seeing the three men, said, "Do you guys want a coke too? It's on me." After distributing the refreshment to all four men, Arthur sat down in the shade to rest. It was then that he noticed the three men with the gasoline can stood stone still with the unopened cokes in their hands.

The guy with the gas can walked to the side of the road and poured the gasoline onto the pavement. "What are you doing?" Arthur asked. "Man, I'm not going to mess with you," the guy replied, "You're a bad dude. I threatened to burn your cross and you don't even flinch. Instead, you offered me a coke."

Arthur, realizing the situation that he had just escaped, replied, "Well, praise the Lord. Do you want to pray with me?"

During the past forty years of carrying the cross, Arthur Blessitt had faced worse situations than this. He was beaten and stoned in Morocco, faced a firing squad in Nicaragua, was choked by the police in LA, attacked with a pistol in Orlando, walked through a minefield in Lebanon, and was thrown by a car bomb in Belfast. He has been arrested 24 times. Surprisingly, the majority of those arrests were in the United States. But this opposition did not stop his journey. He expected resistance from those opposed to the cross. Arthur summarizes his experience. "As we look at the history of mankind we see the walls, the separation, the barriers that have been erected by politicians, by governments, and yes even by religion. But at the cross we see that all people are the same, regardless of their religion, their color."

Less than a year after sending his disciples out to teach, Jesus began to turn toward the cross awaiting Him in Jerusalem. Matthew explained that "Jesus began to show his disciples that he must go to Jerusalem and suffer many things from the elders and chief priests and scribes, and be killed, and on the third day be raised."[1] His disciples had no concept of what was about to happen to Jesus. They saw Jesus' popularity rising, the crowds meeting Him in every town and village, and the miracles He was doing. In their minds, Jesus' success would lead them into positions of power. Some of the disciples even started fighting over who would have the better seat in Jesus' kingdom. So Jesus' prediction of His suffering and death must have hit the disciples like ice water in the face.

Peter decided he needed to correct Jesus and pulled his teacher aside to rebuke Him. "Far be it from you, Lord! This shall never happen to you," Peter declared. Jesus reprimanded him, "Get behind me, Satan! You are a hindrance to me. For you are not setting your mind on the things of God, but on the things of man."[2] Matthew didn't record how Peter responded to being compared with Satan. I am not sure there was anything he could say. He wanted a Jesus who would lead them into Jerusalem in victory and safety, not a leader who would suffer and die. But Jesus knew His path led unavoidably to the cross. This meant that anyone who wanted to follow Him must also face the cross.

After correcting Peter, Jesus turned to His disciples and repeated His earlier words. "If anyone would come after me, let him deny himself and take up his cross and follow me. For whoever would save his life will lose it, but whoever loses his life for my sake will find it." The cross means self-denial. It means losing the life we prefer for the life God has for us.

Self-denial is not something we do well in our modern culture. We are constantly bombarded with messages of self-fulfillment, self-actualization, and self-love. We fight for what we want for ourselves. This spirit is so powerful today that even the symbol of the cross is converted to a symbol of protection or power or might. To wear a cross around your neck, tattoo it on your arm, hang it on your wall, or place it on a hill costs nothing apart from the materials used. It does not cost us ourselves. These are cheap crosses disassociated from the one Jesus is talking about. The cross is a place we go to die—to die to our dreams, our plans, our wisdom, our selfish desires. Only then do we find a life that cannot be lost.

Dr. Martin Luther King, Jr., the preacher who pulled the fiery cross from his front yard, was shot and killed in Memphis on April 4, 1968. There was a point in his life when he realized his work seeking justice for the black community might result in his death. He decided the cost was worth

1. Matthew 16:21
2. Matthew 16:23

the reward. Only a year before his assassination, Dr. King said in a speech, "When I took up the cross, I recognized its meaning . . . The cross is something that you bear, and ultimately that you die on."

According to tradition, all but one of Jesus' disciples (not including Judas who betrayed him) died for their faith. James was executed in Jerusalem a little more than a decade after Jesus' death. It is reported that the executioner, moved by James' courage, became a believer and died alongside him. Thomas was run through with a spear after teaching about Jesus in India. Matthew was stabbed in the back by the king's guard in Ethiopia after confronting King Hertacus. The other James, the first leader of the church in Jerusalem, lived a long life, but was eventually stoned and beaten to death at the age of 94.

The six remaining disciples all died on a cross. Andrew was scourged and tied to a cross to prolong his suffering. He used the two days suspended before his death to preach about Jesus to passersby. Philip was crucified in Hierapolis and Thaddaeus in Edessa, Turkey. Simon the Zealot made it all the way to England before dying on a cross in 74 AD. Bartholomew managed to translate the book of Matthew for locals in India before suffering crucifixion. Only John died peacefully, although exiled, on the island of Patmos. All of Jesus' disciples followed Him, even to the point of taking up their cross and dying.

Peter, the loudmouth leader of his fellow disciples, the one who rebuked his master, eventually came to understand Jesus' words. Witnessing his teacher's death, and then seeing Him after his resurrection, changed Peter's perspective. He later wrote to the early followers of Jesus, "For to this you have been called, because Christ also suffered for you, leaving you an example, so that you might follow in his steps . . . He himself bore our sins in his body on the tree, that we might die to sin and live to righteousness. By his wounds you have been healed."[3] Peter made it to Rome where he was arrested and held by Emperor Nero. When the time came for his execution, Peter requested to be crucified upside down because he was not worthy to die the same way as his Lord. It was a humbled Peter who, after years of carrying his cross, laid it down to die on one.

What does this mean for today? Does following Jesus mean you have to die for him? Maybe. More followers of Jesus are dying for their faith in the world today than any other time in history. However, that is not the full meaning of carrying the cross. To take up your cross is to die to

3. 1 Peter 2:21, 24

yourself while you are still alive. It is following Jesus wherever, whenever, and whatever that means. It probably doesn't mean carrying a twelve foot cross around the globe, but it does mean being willing to.

The cross can be divisive, but the more followers of Jesus who carry it in their hearts with humility and love, the more the true meaning of the cross will shine through. Arthur Blessitt recently explained why he carries his wooden cross. "One of the most important missions I've had in this forty-year journey has been reinterpreting the cross. For centuries, Muslims have been in conflict with the cross. And yet I carried the cross openly in every Muslim nation on earth. Through the smiles, through the love, through the message that in the cross the worst of man met the best of God and that God cares for us. They saw it in a new way, or I wouldn't be alive today."

16.

New Priorities

"Thou hast made us for thyself, O Lord, and our heart is restless
until it finds its rest in thee."

—AUGUSTINE OF HIPPO, CONFESSIONS

I RETURNED TO BELGRADE, to Sanja and Jovana, the same, but also different. I started regularly visiting a church on Sundays as well as regularly
reading the Bible. My priorities, my habits, and my behavior started to
change. Until then, swear words were every other word out of my mouth,
overnight I stopped swearing. Sanja noticed the change in me, and she liked
it. I began to pray every morning. I would get to work earlier to start the day
with prayer and reading the New Testament.

One morning while I was praying, I felt God say to me I should return
to BiH, to Mostar, to serve Him there and to tell others about His love and
grace. As soon as that thought crossed my mind, I dismissed it. Sanja and I
had sworn to each other we would never return to BiH. We were too hurt
by the war and everything surrounding it. Besides, in BiH there is a war
almost every fifty years. My father's great aunt, Staka, who lived to be 93,
survived five wars, rebellions, and armed uprisings during her lifetime; my
mother went through two wars . . . we didn't want our children to grow up
in that environment. We had a better plan, we wanted to leave for a foreign
country.

When we were facing administrative complications with a new work
permit in Cyprus, we decided to try for an immigrant visa to America,
Canada, or Australia. The further away, the better. But when we shared

those plans with my father's cousin in Belgrade, Vera and her husband Filip talked us out of it. They were only children in a childless marriage, and we were their closest relatives. They were well off, with an enormous house in Dedinje (an elite part of Belgrade), land on the seaside, a weekend house in the mountains, and a large bank account. At that time they were in their late sixties. They told us there was no need for us to go abroad and to struggle our whole lives to make a life for ourselves, when we could stay and care for them when they got older, and then we would inherit all they had. It seemed like a good plan to us, so we stayed in Belgrade.

First we had sworn not to return to Mostar, and then an inheritance was promised us in Belgrade, but now I had that strange feeling that God wanted me to go back. I tried to put the thought out of my mind, but no matter how hard I tried, it wouldn't leave. I decided to ask God to clearly show me if this thought was really from Him, and He did just that. I prayed and told God that if it was His will for us to return to Mostar, then he could provide the money we needed to move in a miraculous way. I was specific with the amount.

That same day, on the sidewalk, I found a wallet with the exact amount for which I prayed. There was only money in the wallet, no documents. There was no longer a dilemma. God wanted me to return to Mostar. But I didn't want to. So I prayed that He would be the Lord of my life, "not my will, but Your will Lord." And then again, a phone call changed everything. They told me that my mother's sickness had suddenly returned, that they had urgently sent her to a hospital in Zagreb, and that if I wanted to see her, I needed to travel there.

During the summer, the doctors had been more than amazed at my mom's recovery. The leukemia was in total remission, and the diagnosis was especially good, and now this awful news, this bucket of cold water. My sister and I agreed to meet in Mostar and travel together to Zagreb. I paid for a ticket to Sarajevo, one taxi to the demarcation line, another to the station, and another bus to Mostar. It was sunrise when the bus left Sarajevo via Ilidža toward Mostar. The sun began to appear from behind Mount Trebević in the cold November sky, as sunlight and fog played on the bus window. All at once I felt God's presence in that bus. I felt it was an important moment, that God wanted to tell me something, but I didn't know what. I looked at my watch, it was a little after 7:00 a.m. After a couple of hours on the bus, I arrived in Mostar, and walked across the Carinski Bridge to my sister's apartment. There I found my sister and her family crying, having just heard, as they told me at the door, that Mom was dead. I asked them if she died a little after seven that morning. It was unclear to them how I knew. It was unclear to me as well.

The following days we were very busy organizing the transfer of the body from Croatia to Mostar and organizing the funeral. When Pastor Karmelo came to arrange the details of the funeral, I told him I thought we should read a verse from the Bible, John 3:16, at the funeral: "For God so loved the world that he gave his only Son that whoever believes in him should not perish, but have eternal life." I didn't understand why tears welled up in his eyes.

Sanja came with Jovana from Belgrade for the funeral. The funeral was a unique experience: Bjelušine Cemetery where my father is buried, large funeral, lots of people, many tears, and the church choir behind me singing one of my mom's favorite songs: " . . . I know that God has made a way for me . . . " And in my heart was a perfect peace, a supernatural peace, a peace that this world does not give. I didn't have any sadness at all. I almost felt guilty I wasn't sad, for my mother had died, and I was at her funeral. But I knew she was in a better place; I knew she was in heaven with her Savior. While they lowered her casket into the ground, my gaze was fixed in the distance, fixed on heaven from which I steadfastly await my Savior.

We decided to stay in Mostar, where God wanted us. Our cousins in Belgrade weren't happy and let us know clearly that the deal with the inheritance was off. We were prepared to pay the price. Sanja, even though she was from a religious, traditional Catholic family, still hadn't decided to accept Jesus as her Lord and Savior. She knew about Him, but she didn't know Him. The Evangelical Church of BiH was a minority community, and in a war-torn city where ethnic and religious tensions were enormous, it was quickly labeled a sect. In their ignorance, people started to spread lies and misinformation. Sanja's parents heard these stories and started pressuring her, and through her, me. This all affected our marriage. Sanja began to cave in under the pressure and those changes she saw in me were no longer so precious.

The woman, whom I had asked to take off her cross earrings and stop going to church so we could start dating, was now against me going to church. Once she even asked me why I wasn't like other "normal" men who go to cafes. Why did I have to go to church? The tensions grew so great I started to worry about our marriage. I began to pray every day that she would accept Jesus, repent from her sin, and make peace with God. I talked with her, and sometimes even "pushed" her too much, but she didn't want to go to a church service. A Christian band visited the church, and we organized a concert with them. I invited Sanja and, after convincing her they wouldn't preach but just play, she decided to come with me. The songs were Christian and between songs the members of the band shared briefly about God, His love and grace, and about Jesus' sacrifice on the cross.

At one point, the singer suggested we pray in pairs. I prayed with a friend next to me then started looking around the auditorium for Sanja. I saw her in another corner of the room with Sanela, a member of the church, praying for one another—tears were streaming down her face. I knew that she had finally met the Savior, and that she had decided to follow Him. I couldn't have been happier. Things changed overnight; the fights stopped, and love, joy, and peace entered our home. Sanja decided to be baptized by immersion, which I had already done, and decided to share the news with her parents.

Even though we knew their attitude toward the Evangelical Church, we were still shocked by their reaction. They told Sanja that if she got baptized, she was no longer their daughter, and they didn't want to hear from her anymore. Sanja calmly, gently, and lovingly told them that she had decided to follow Jesus and nothing could change that, that she was sorry about their decision, that she hoped they would change their minds, and that she was always there for them. Sanja was baptized, and for months after the baptism her parents didn't want any contact with us. Contact started again when our son David was born. Today, eighteen years later, our relationship with them is much better; we visit each other regularly and we continue to pray they will accept Jesus as their Lord and Savior.

When we returned to Mostar, along with volunteer work in the church, I started to look for a job. I refused an offer to work in a casino, and was hired, instead, by a restaurant. Along with working, I began attending Bible School. Sanja became pregnant, and on November 11, 1999, our son, David Dragan, came into the world. He was named after King David and my father, Dragan. When Sanja was a little girl she had bad scoliosis, and had to wear a medical brace that looked more like a medieval-torture device than a medical device. The brace was tightened around the hips, and because Sanja was in puberty at the time her hips stayed narrow and couldn't open enough for labor and delivery. The doctor noticed this toward the end of her pregnancy with Jovana, which was why Jovana had to be delivered by cesarean section.

During her pregnancy with David, two doctors in Mostar confirmed the same thing. The cesarean section was scheduled for the end of November, but a few days before, Sanja suddenly had unexpected labor pains in the early morning hours. Rain was coming down in buckets, it was two in the morning, and because I didn't have my own car, I ran through the dark and cold, soaked to the bone, to the church to get the church's van. I had the keys with me, but the van was parked in front of the church because I didn't expect Sanja to have labor pains that night. We had planned everything, conferred with the doctors, and in prayer brought everything to the Lord. There was no room for mistakes. And now this. I was angry at God, and as I ran, soaking wet, I was complaining to Him and asking if He had forgotten us.

I brought the van, took Jovana from her bed, and settled her and Sanja in the van. I hurried to the hospital, which wasn't far away, where we realized, to our disappointment, that the doctor on call was the one we didn't like at all. That's all we needed; it was the last straw. I left Sanja, completely disappointed, and returned home, placed Jovana in bed, put on some water for coffee and sat down to pray. At that moment the phone rang. I answered it and on the other end of the line was Sanja, speaking in a completely normal voice. I thought she had forgotten to take something, so I asked her what I needed to bring her, to which she replied that she had given birth to a son by natural childbirth, and that everything was alright.

I was confident she was joking because it couldn't have been more than 20–30 minutes since I left her, and this was her first natural delivery (Jovana was delivered by c-section). Three doctors, one in Belgrade and two in Mostar said that if she gave birth naturally it would be a difficult birth and dangerous for her and the baby. When she convinced me she wasn't joking, I realized God was in control, and our prayers did not go unanswered, but that His plans were different and, as usual, much better than our plans. I repented and I learned another important life lesson, one that can't be forgotten.

17.

The Sign of the Cross

"Hoc Signo Victor Eris—in this sign, conquer"

FOR THE FIRST TIME, Constantine was insecure about the future. He had not faced much difficulty taking Northern Italy from the usurper Maxentius that spring, but those victories did not give Constantine solace on October 27, 312 AD as he camped on the banks of the Tiber River. Across the flowing waters lay the fortified city of Rome and, within the city, Maxentius with 100,000 troops. Neither Severus, who was Caesar under Constantine's father, nor Galerius, who had all the might of the Eastern Empire, succeeded in unseating Maxentius. Yet that was what Constantine, at twenty-four years of age, and his 40,000 men, were preparing to do. The signs were not good. Word reached Constantine that Maxentius, faithful to the old cults, received a good omen from the Sibylline books. They foretold the imminent destruction of a great enemy of Rome. With joy and confidence, the sitting Caesar proceeded to celebrate the sixth anniversary of his rule with public games.

Constantine knew he needed some aid greater than military strength. How could he defeat the larger army of Maxentius as well as the pagan deities that supported him? The thought occurred to him that his predecessors had followed the pantheon of gods, giving them sacrifices and offerings, and yet all of them came to an unhappy end without even a warning from those gods. Meanwhile, his father, Constantius, who believed in one supreme God above all others and refused to persecute the Christians under his rule, reigned successfully and died happy. Constantine knew what he needed to do. At midday, while Maxentius basked in the roar of the games,

Constantine lifted his eyes to the sky and implored the "Highest Deity" to reveal himself and help him through this trial.

As he did, Constantine saw "the trophy of a cross of light in the heavens, above the sun, and bearing the inscription *Hoc Signo Victor Eris*"—in this sign conquer.

For the Romans, the cross was a symbol of pain, shame, and death. The great orator Cicero said, "the very word 'cross' should be far removed not only from the person of a Roman citizen but from his thoughts, his eyes and his ears." Yet, this was the sign under which Constantine was to march. Understandably, he was confused. That evening, as he later recounted to the church historian Eusebius, Constantine had a dream. "In his sleep the Christ of God appeared to him with the same sign which he had seen in the heavens, and commanded him to make a likeness of that sign which he had seen in the heavens, and to use it as a safeguard in all engagements with his enemies." At dawn, Constantine sent for those in his camp familiar with the Christian faith, and asked them to explain his revelation. They told him the sign was "the symbol of immortality" and a trophy of victory over death, won by Christ's act on the cross. They might have also told him how believers were marked at baptism by the sign of the cross and that that very same sign, invoked in the name of Christ, could protect believers against the forces of evil. Constantine had found his battle standard—a symbol more powerful than the omens of Maxentius, a symbol to inspire courage in his men, a symbol to lead him to victory.

Constantine's craftsman prepared a new battle standard. It was made of a long pole with a horizontal cross beam, all coated in gold. Above the cross-bar was a golden crown of laurels at the center of which were the Greek letters chi (X) and rho (P)—the first two letters in the name Christ—one interposed on the other. This was the Christogram. From the cross-beam hung a silken fabric woven with jewels and embroidered with the images of the Imperial family.

Constantine recounted his vision to his men and commanded them to bear the *caeleste signum Dei*, the heavenly sign of God. Pulling blackened sticks from the previous night's fire, the soldiers marked their shields with the Christogram (XP). Most of the warriors did not understand what the letters meant, but sought protection under the sign of their commander. Thus prepared, the men turned to face the Aurelian Walls of Rome and the most powerful army on earth.

While Constantine was looking to the heavens, Maxentius was looking to the people of Rome. During the games held in honor of his anniversary, the notoriously vocal crowd taunted the ruler chanting, "Constantine cannot be conquered!" Maxentius, confident in his omen but unsure how long the people of Rome would stand behind him in a siege, made a fateful decision. Instead of remaining in the city, as he did against Severus and Galerius, he brought his men outside the city to meet Constantine's army. Maxentius had cut the Milvian bridge to prevent his enemy from approaching the walls. In order to reach the invading forces across the Tiber, he lashed boats together and topped them with planks. In this way, Maxentius positioned his troops on the far side of the river, backs to Rome and shields toward the invaders.

Constantine's cavalry, emboldened by their new standard, charged that of Maxentius, breaking their lines in short order. Then the infantry, stretching the length of the Roman lines, moved forward. Maxentius' men were pinned between the slashing swords of Constantine and the flowing currents of the Tiber. Those who were not cut down were driven into the waters to meet their end. Maxentius managed to hold his ground until Constantine himself led a cavalry assault. Maxentius fled back toward the walls of Rome. In the melee, he was knocked from the makeshift boat bridge, fell headlong into the Tiber, and sank to the bottom under the weight of his armor. His body was later found washed up on the far shore, a victim of his avarice and fear.

Both Pagan and Christian historians of that era attribute divine influence to the downfall of Maxentius. Why did Maxentius leave the safety of the walled city? The panegyrics note, "The Divine Mind . . . snatched wisdom away from the abominable man so that . . . he suddenly rushed out and . . . sealed the very day of his accession with his final destruction." Why did Maxentius cross the river and leave his men trapped with water at their backs? A Christian historian wrote, "God himself drew the tyrant as if by secret cords a long way outside the gates."

When Constantine entered Rome, the victorious general, he was preceded by two symbols: the *labarum* with its golden cross and Christogram and a second spear on which rested the head of Maxentius.

Modern historians debate the historicity of Constantine's vision and the authenticity of his conversion to Christianity. Did Constantine, under the strain of the impending battle, hallucinate the heavenly vision? Did he fabricate events in order to motivate his men and gain power? Or did he have a true encounter with the living God? However these questions are answered, it is undeniable that Constantine's ascension and rule changed the position of Christianity in the Roman Empire and transformed the meaning of the cross in the minds of its citizens. The cross—the means of the most shameful punishment reserved for the lowest of criminals—became the symbol of victory and power. Four months after the battle of Milvian Bridge, Constantine reversed centuries of Christian persecution throughout the Roman Empire with the Edict of Milan. Beyond that, he donated one of the palaces from the Imperial estates to the Bishop of Rome so that his residence would be congruent with the importance of his status. In 316, when Constantine marched out against the Eastern Empire, Licinius' men came to fear the *labarum* and the mystical courage it gave the men surrounding it. Even Roman money began to bear the mark of the cross. This is a far cry from the ideas of guilt, pain, and ignominy formerly associated with the cross.

In honor of Constantine's victory in Rome, a giant statue of the Emperor was placed in the western apse of the Basilica of Maxentius, the largest building in the Roman Forum. The figure of an enthroned Constantine stood forty feet tall, his head alone 8 feet long. His eyes looked upward, and his right hand pointed to the heavens. In his left hand was the *labarum*—a cross and Christogram in the center of Rome. At his feet were inscribed the words, "Through this sign of salvation, which is the true symbol of goodness, I rescued your city and freed it from the tyrant's yoke . . . " However, in freeing the city under the sign of the cross, Constantine entangled the symbol of goodness with the tyranny of the sword.

18.

Victory or Failure?

"Long lasting victory can never be separated from a long lasting stand on the foundation of the cross."

—WATCHMAN NEE

TODAY'S ROME IS FILLED with many historical places, such as the catacombs, Trevi Fountain, the Vatican, St. Peter's Basilica, and the magnificent Colosseum. A few thousand years after the Colosseum was built, visitors can't remain indifferent before the magnificence and beauty of this architectural masterpiece. In this place, they held gladiator battles, games, and spectacles lasting for days after the triumphal processions marking great military victories and wars won. Right beside the Colosseum is the Arch of Constantine, the largest and most decorated triumphal arch of the ancient era. It was erected after the Battle of Milvian Bridge and the triumph of Constantine's troops. The triumphal parade passed through the city's streets and through the arches that marked earlier great battles and victories.

These Roman Triumphs were civil, military, and religious manifestations, which no one in Rome wanted to miss. To organize a Triumph the Roman Senate needed to approve it, and they did so only after a great military victory in which the opposing army was completely destroyed losing no less than 5000 men, after a battle in which the Roman Empire conquered a vast new territory, or after a successful war when the legions could return to Rome.

After the Roman Senate proclaimed a Triumph, the general would come with his army and encamp on Campus Martius in front of the walls of Rome to await the completion of preparations for the Triumph. The day of the procession began with speeches by the military leaders addressing the Senate, citizens, and soldiers. Afterwards, the triumphal procession formed outside the city and entered through *Porta Triumphalis*, which was only used for this purpose. The Roman Triumph moved through the streets of Rome along a route chosen by the military leaders. At the head of the procession were consuls and politicians, behind them musicians playing trumpets and fanfare, and then flag bearers, followed by cages of wild animals from the area where the war was fought, and then the spoils of war—the more silver and gold the better. After the spoils came the captives, preferably military leaders, officers, nobles, and kings . . . often chained—a symbol of complete defeat. People mocked them and laughed at them. They were losers, a symbol of their nation's destruction, a symbol not only of lost battles but of a lost war. On chariots they pulled large paintings of the fortified cities they had conquered, and sometimes, in the middle of the procession, they would kill some of the captives to illustrate the victory.

After the captives came *lictors*, or military bodyguards, who carried laurel wreaths, and after them, in decorated combat chariots pulled by four horses or sometimes four trained deer, came the General, the star of the Roman Triumph, the victor. He wore a laurel crown on his head and held laurel branches in his left hand and in his right hand an ivory specter with an eagle on the tip—a symbol of victory.

Next to the General on the chariot stood a slave holding a gold crown above his head the whole time and whispering in his ear the words "look behind you and remember that you are only a man" (*Respice post te! Hominem te memento!*), so that the General, surrounded by such glorious honor, would not think himself a god. After the General's combat chariot, there was his family on horseback, then the officers, and then, at the very end of the procession, the army singing victory songs.

The Roman Triumph circled the whole city, finally arriving at the Temple of Jupiter Capitolinus where they slaughtered oxen and offered them as sacrifices. Because the Romans were pagans and polytheists, the Triumphs passed by many temples dedicated to many deities in which they burned frankincense and other incenses. The whole city was filled with the aromas wafting up from the temples. Those aromas reminded the victors of their victories, and the captives of their defeat and certain ruin. Some of the captives ended up as slaves, some were killed in jail, and some were forced to end their lives in the spectacles and gladiatorial games held in the

Colosseum during the days that followed. The same aroma was to some a reminder of victory, and to others, defeat.

In contrast to the Roman Triumph that was a symbol of victory and victors, the cross was a symbol of suffering, death, pain, and loss. To the cross they nailed the worst criminals, the ones they wanted to brutally punish. The person on the cross died over the course of hours, sometimes days, in the worst agony and suffering. Can the cross be a symbol of victory? Maybe for the executioners, but what about for those who hung on the cross? What about Jesus? If Jesus died such an awful, tortuous death, how is it possible the Bible says that Jesus canceled "the record of debt that stood against us with its legal demands. This he set aside, nailing it to the cross. He disarmed the rulers and authorities and put them to open shame, by triumphing over them in him . . . "[1]?

What is Paul talking about here? Didn't Jesus hang on the cross? Didn't He die on it? How can He be a victor? To find the answer to this question, we must remember the chapter "Necessary or Unnecessary?" in which we talked about the problem of sin. All people are sinful and sin separates us from God, disobedience to God hinders our relationship with Him, and the consequences are God's vengeance, but God loves us and wants to help us. He gave us free will to make choices, we misuse that free will, make the wrong choices, and we mess up, yet He loves us and wants to have fellowship with us, to give us a second chance.

We have already spoken about the Old Testament system of animal sacrifice in which the sacrificial animal needed to pay for the sins of the man who was sacrificing it. We also mentioned how the book of Hebrews teaches that these animal sacrifices weren't perfect; all they could really accomplish was to remind people that they were sinful and that sin has serious consequences. And what did God do to help people?

God decided to become a man, to "insert" Himself as an embryo in the womb of a young girl, Mary, to be born exactly like us except for sin, to live a life as we do, to be tempted in every way, only without sinning. They nailed Him to the cross, not because of His sin, but because of ours. He died an awful tortuous death in pain and suffering. In the hardest moments, He even felt forgotten and forsaken by His Father. He died, and yielded up His soul! Victory or defeat?

In the Gospel of Matthew, it is written that at the moment of Jesus' death the earth shook, rocks split, and the temple curtain tore in two from

1. Colossians 2:14–15

top to bottom.[2] The temple in the Old Testament symbolized the place of God's presence; the temple curtain separated the Holy of Holies from the rest of the temple. People were allowed in the rest of the temple, but only the High Priest could go behind the curtain into the Holy of Holies and then only once a year to pray for the people's forgiveness. When he entered, they would tie a rope to his leg, so that if he died behind the curtain, they could pull him out; no one dared go behind the curtain into the place of God's presence.

The problem was sin, this sin with which we are all "infected," and which separates us from God. Jesus conquered sin through His death on the cross. Until that moment there was no solution for the problem of sin, but since Jesus' death a solution exists! That's why the curtain was torn: the obstacle to gain access to God was taken away, the victory over sin was won, the people needed only to accept Jesus as their Lord and Savior. He died to save us from the vengeance and the consequences of sin. All you need to do after you understand it intellectually is to accept Him as Savior, to tell Him, "Jesus, I confess that I'm a sinner, and I'm aware that my sin separates me from You. Thank You that You died to pay the price and take onto yourself the punishment for my sins. Be my Savior." But that is not enough. You need to accept Him as Lord, like I did in Mostar in the darkness of my room, to tell Him, "Jesus I surrender my life into Your hands. I want to follow You and to do Your will in life. Be my Lord."

If Jesus' death on the cross was the end of the story, it wouldn't be a victorious one, but His death was not the end, it was only the beginning. After the Roman soldiers were convinced that Jesus was dead, they laid His body in a tomb, sealed the entrance with a large stone, and set a Roman guard to watch over the tomb. But neither death, nor stone, nor Roman guard could stop God's plan and purpose from being fulfilled. As He promised, Jesus rose again on the third day. The women that came to the graveyard found an empty tomb. During the next forty days, Jesus regularly met with the disciples, talking and eating with them. He was in a resurrected body, and Thomas, who didn't believe when he heard that Jesus was resurrected, was allowed to touch the wounds on His hands and side. One time He even entered a room through closed doors.

Throughout those forty days, hundreds of people saw Him in dozens of different places.

2. Matthew 27:31

At the time the New Testament was written, the majority of the witnesses were alive. Jesus' resurrection is an historical and legally verifiable fact. But even this isn't the end. After forty days Jesus ascended, in front of the disciples, taken up into the air, into the clouds, before their eyes.[3] Jesus had foretold to His disciples that after His resurrection He would go to His Father in heaven to prepare a place for His followers. The angels present at His ascension told the disciples Jesus would come again. The Bible teaches us that Jesus will come for his faithful to take them to their eternal home in heaven where they will delight in God forever, where there will be no more sadness, nor pain, nor sin, nor sickness, nor war, nor deceit . . . That's the victory, the victory that Jesus won on the cross!

That's why the Bible uses the picture of the Roman Triumph, "He (Jesus) disarmed the rulers and authorities and put them to open shame, by triumphing over them in him."[4] These rulers and authorities are the same ones the Bible talks about in the Epistle to Ephesians 6, not worldly rulers, but the devil and evil spirits who abide in heavenly places, and whose plan of death, destruction and eternal separation from God was thwarted by Jesus through His death on the cross. However, the "war" still rages, and the devil still has certain powers on earth.

If we look around us, if we read the newspaper or watch the news on TV, we will quickly come to the same conclusion. But the victory is assured, and the triumphal procession with Jesus in His "combat chariot" is guaranteed. Nothing, absolutely nothing can bring this into question. When Jesus comes again, when He comes for His followers, the triumphal procession will begin, and the devil and those who haven't accepted Jesus go to their doom, while those who have accepted Jesus as their Lord and Savior will go to heaven, to the heavenly city where we will spend an eternity with the Lord.

Like it says in the first letter to the Corinthians, "'Death is swallowed up in victory [on the cross]. O death, where is your victory? O death, where is your sting?' The sting of death is sin, and the power of sin is the law. But thanks be to God, who gives us the victory through our Lord Jesus Christ."[5] Second Corinthians also uses a picture of the triumphal procession, "But thanks be to God, who in Christ always leads us in triumphal procession, and through us spreads the fragrance of the knowledge of him

3. Acts 1

4. Colossians 2:15

5. 1 Corinthians 15:54b–57

everywhere. For we are the aroma of Christ to God among those who are being saved and among those who are perishing, to one a fragrance from death to death, to the other a fragrance from life to life . . . "[6]

Just as in ancient Rome the wafting aroma of the sacrifices during the triumphal procession were a reminder to people, to some of victory, and to others of defeat and impending doom, so we as believers spread an "aroma" that reminds us of the victory won on the cross, a reminder to some of salvation, and to others of condemnation. In which group are you? It's not too late to make a decision for Jesus.

6. 2 Corinthians 2:14–16

19.

The Storm after the Calm

"That's just what we need. Before we recognized that there are problems, we didn't have to solve them."

—DUŠKO RADOVIĆ

DURING SANJA'S SECOND PREGNANCY I was hired in a restaurant in Mostar. I worked, and we could live from my salary. We went to church regularly, helped with ministry activities, drove older people to services in the church van, distributed humanitarian aid, and attended prayer meetings and Bible studies. The young man that led the humanitarian work for the church had an opportunity to go abroad for school, and his job was left vacant. Pastor Karmelo and his wife, Ivon, invited Sanja and me to dinner and offered me the job working in the church, leading the humanitarian work through the organization "Agape." That was the same humanitarian organization from which my mother had received help for my sister's newborn baby during the war and the reason she started going to church and decided to follow Jesus.

The word *agape* in ancient Greek is a word for "love," and not just any kind of love, but unconditional love—a love that doesn't ask for anything in return. I liked the idea, and I wanted to serve the Lord and help people in my town through "Agape." This was right after the war, and the needs were still great. The only problem was that the pay the pastor offered was quite a bit less than my paycheck at the restaurant, and the pay from the restaurant was just enough for us to get through each month. Besides that, Sanja was going to give birth soon, which meant our living expenses would automatically increase. About the same time, I received a job offer from Elektrodistribucija, the public electric utility, a state firm with large and secure salaries, social and health insurance, and a pension fund. I didn't have any of this in the restaurant, and the church didn't have the money to pay for insurance. After talking to Sanja and praying together, we believed I should accept the job in the church. If it was really from God, He would care for our family and provide for our needs. I quit my job in the restaurant, turned down the job in Elektrodistribucija, and started working at the church.

There were days when we didn't know how we were going to buy food the next day or pay our bills, but God always took care of us in some unexpected way so that we were neither hungry, nor thirsty, nor in debt to anyone. In addition to receiving and distributing humanitarian aid, I was helping more and more in the church in other spiritual ways. We started a Bible study group for married couples in our home, I organized men's meetings, sometimes led prayer meetings, was involved in evangelistic activities of the church, and sometimes the pastor asked me to preach. I had started going to Bible school while I was still working in the restaurant and in two years, I finished a four-year program. After that I was chosen at a church members' meeting to be the assistant pastor and an elder in the church. I preached more often, and when the pastor was away, I led the church.

The next few years went by, life settled down, there weren't any major snags, our relationship with Sanja's parents started mending, people in the church loved us and we loved them, and Jovana started to school . . . Then we received an offer from the elders of the Evangelical Church of BiH and Pastor John Rowell to move to Sarajevo to take over the leadership of a church John's organization had started and that was now having some major problems. We had already built a safe place in Mostar, so we didn't want to go anywhere. We had an apartment I had inherited from my parents, my sister and her family were there, as well as Sanja's parents with whom we had just started to build a relationship again, Jovana had already made friends in school, the church was one of the largest in BiH, and it was good working under Karmelo's leadership . . . also West Mostar was mostly Catholic and Sarajevo was a mostly Muslim city.

After a short time of consideration and prayer, in which we did not really listen to God's voice, we rejected the offer. But God had a different plan, and He didn't give us peace about this decision at all. Four months after we rejected the offer, we were in a car packed with our stuff on the way to Sarajevo, heading toward a new chapter God had for us and our lives.

Soon after our arrival in Sarajevo, a couple of events confirmed that the move was God's will. The situation in which we found ourselves was complicated and in no way easy, so that it was necessary for all concerned to start over again. We didn't start from the ground up, but from underground. Immediately after we arrived, we officially registered the church under the name "The Evangelical Church of Koševsko Brdo," named after the part of town where the church was located. The good thing, at the very beginning, was we were not alone; we had a few co-laborers from John's organization.

John raised funds in America for the purchase of a building, and God led us to the right building, so after only a few months, we had a registered church, a building that we needed to renovate to our needs, and a few co-workers. Slowly but surely the church started to grow. Only a few months after our arrival we had our first baptism; three people were baptized. Even though there weren't a lot of us, we had a wide spectrum of activities. In addition to regular Sunday services, prayer meetings, and Bible studies, we also did humanitarian aid, children's ministry, puppet shows, sports ministry, foreign language courses, etc.

After a few years, life settled down. The church was growing slowly but surely, we had to even renovate the sanctuary because it had become too small. Jovana found new friends at school and, three years after moving, David started school. We decided to sell our apartment in Mostar, the one I inherited from my parents, and buy an apartment in Sarajevo. At the beginning of December 2007, we moved into our new apartment in Vogošća, a suburb of Sarajevo.

Just when we had all the pieces in place, we had a shock. In February 2008, I noticed some specific problems with my health, and after consultation with Dr. Maja, a member of our church and a good friend, I went to a specialist who gave me a diagnosis—testicular cancer. Shock! My father died of cancer when he was 39 years old, and my grandfather died of cancer in his last thirties . . . I thought history was repeating itself. I was ready to meet my Maker, and I wasn't afraid of death because I knew where I was going, to heaven with Jesus. I knew that on the cross He paid for my sins, that I am justified and forgiven, but I wasn't ready to leave Sanja and my children.

After the initial shock wore off, I wrote to all my friends around the world asking them to pray for me. I had an operation to remove the tumor and I went through radiation. The prognosis was good because it was discovered in the early stages. Through these difficulties, these problems, I saw how my priorities in life were mixed up, how minute, unimportant things stole my joy and my time. I learned some important life lessons, and I was thankful that God brought me through it all. The first three years I had check-ups every three months. The check-ups were always stressful; I couldn't wait for three years to pass so I wouldn't have to go every three months.

Just after the third year, I got a sharp pain in my right kidney that was so strong I couldn't even get up to go to the doctor. When the pain subsided a little that afternoon, I somehow made my way to the doctor who sent me to the hospital where they diagnosed me with a kidney stone. It took two months for them to realize they were wrong and diagnose me with cancer in the abdominal cavity. Again, shock! Why Lord? Why again? This time was harder for me than the first. I thought I was healed, that it was all behind me, but then I received much worse news: the tumor was large, the size of a fist and next to one of the vena cava, so an operation wasn't possible. I sought a second opinion and a third—all the doctors said the same thing. The only thing left was to try chemotherapy and a heavy dose of it. Five days a week, every day, I had a needle in my arm for eight hours, as a gallon of different drugs and liquids ran through my veins, and then a two-week break for my body to recover.

When I came for the second cycle, the number of leukocytes (white blood cells) was too low to continue the treatment. The normal number is between $4–11$ x109 /L and the minimum to continue the treatment is 3 x109 /L. My blood levels were 2.7. The doctor wanted to delay the treatment for seven days, but at my insistence she agreed to send me to the lab to check my leukocytes level again. She knew I was a Christian and I told her that we were praying and that we believed God was all-powerful, but she was skeptical since the test results were only two days old. She said we couldn't expect anything would significantly change in only two days.

I told Sanja to pray and I left for the lab. While I went I prayed, "God, please make the number of leukocytes jump to 2.9 and then I will talk her into continuing the treatment." I didn't have the faith for 3 x109 /L. They took my blood and told me to wait for twenty minutes. The results arrived, I took them through the opening at the counter, and when I looked couldn't believe it, 7.7 x109 /L. I'm not a big supporter of biblical numerology, but I know that the number seven in the Bible means completeness. God created the world in six days and then on the seventh day he rested, so 7.7 was a sign from God to me! I ran, or better said jumped, to the doctor's office, and, full of joy, bounded inside. The doctor was surprised, but she said, "It happens sometimes," forgetting that just a half hour before she had said we shouldn't expect any changes in such a short time.

That miracle gave me some wind beneath my wings, and my attitude toward my situation completely changed because God reminded me He was in control. After the second cycle, the doctor decided to do an MRI to see if the tumor was responding to the chemotherapy. They put me in the machine, closed the door of the room, and the process began: breathe, don't breathe, machine sounds, knocking, clanging, the voice of the technician in the speakers again, breathe in, hold your breath, breathe out, just breathe . . . then a long break, and it started all over again.

This was not my first MRI, however this time it seemed to last forever. In the end when they opened the door and the technician removed me from the machine, I asked the doctor if everything was okay, and why the process lasted so long. She excitedly informed me that there wasn't a trace of the tumor, and that they were confused by its absence so they repeated the whole process to see if they had done something wrong. Praise God! Today, as I write this, it's been six years and eight months since my last chemotherapy. After five years I was medically declared cancer free.

Through these difficult health problems and hardships, I learned many lessons. I realized, even though I knew this intellectually before, that things aren't always how we want them to be. Not every prayer is answered in the way we want it to be, but God has His reasons, and He knows what's best for us. All we need to do is trust Him.

When I was first diagnosed with cancer nine full years ago, I prayed one of the stupidest prayers of my life. I prayed, "Lord, give me just five more years to live!" I'm thankful to God that He didn't answer that prayer. Again, He had a better plan!

20.

The Shame of the Cross

Deus Christianorum Onochoetes
"The God of the Christians—born of an ass."
—INSCRIPTION ON AN IMAGE PUBLISHED
IN CARTHAGE CIRCA 197 AD

THE YOUNG MAN LIVED at the southwest foot of the Palatine Hill in Rome, a building wedged between the palatial structures of Emperor Septimius Severus and the Circus Maximus. He was fortunate. Few foreign slaves had the opportunities afforded him in the *paedagogium*, a training school for imperial servants. He was learning Latin and Greek and some of the arts. As a servant in the courts of the emperor, Alexamenos needed to excel not only in beauty, but also in knowledge and speech.

Alexamenos was not alone in the school, although it often seemed that way. Nationality was not what set him apart—there were many other Greek slaves in training. It was his faith. Alexamenos was a part of a religious sect despised by the Romans for its backwards ways and stubborn insistence on rejecting proper worship. He was a Christian. And everyone in the *paedagogium* knew it now. There was a corridor that ran the length of the school building through which all the boys passed daily. Scratched into the plaster was graffiti of the kind you would find in any bathroom or boys school. But in the alcove at the center of the corridor there appeared a new inscription. On the left, a person is depicted wearing a *colobium*, the shortened, sleeveless tunic of a slave. His face is lifted to the right, and he is raising his hand to his lips as if blowing a kiss. The object of his gaze is to his immediate right. This second caricature, also wearing a *colobium,* is raised up on a T-shaped cross, arms outstretched along the horizontal beam. The most striking feature of this "person" is his head. He has the head of a donkey. Scratched below the drawings are the Greek words, Αλεξαμενος σεβετε θεον, "Alexamenos worships [his] god."

The Alexamenos Graffito, which was discovered in 1857 and now resides in the Palatine Antiquarium Museum, is regarded by most scholars as the earliest surviving depiction of Jesus. Dated to the beginning of the 3rd century, it is also the oldest pictorial representation of Jesus' crucifixion. The fact that the earliest known "crucifix" was scratched into the wall of a boy's school in order to mock a Christian is revealing. The cross was not yet the sign of victory it became under Constantine. It was a symbol of mockery and shame.

The "artist" was intentional in his work, positioning the characters for maximum effect. The ass-man on the cross is viewed from behind, a perspective of derision. The short, unbelted tunic he wears leaves his legs bare and marks him as a foreigner or slave. At the time, the more expensive and enveloping *toga* was worn only by respectable Roman citizens as a sign of wealth and prestige. No such respect is afforded the creature on the cross. The raised hand of the second figure, Alexamenos, is also meant for derision. When the Romans visited the temple of their god, they would perform a ceremonial kiss in expression of worship. Pliny the Elder described the process, "In veneration, we kiss the right hand and we bring [it] back around the whole body." This is what Alexamenos appears to be doing in the drawing, except he is using his left hand. It is as if the artist is saying, "Alexamenos is so backwards he doesn't even know what hand to use in worshipping his god."

Of course, the most obvious insult in the drawing is the object of Alexamenos' worship. It has the head of a donkey. Tertullian, a Christian apologist writing at the end of the 2nd century, tells of a "new representation of our god" recently publicized in his city. He describes a freelance animal fighter who walked through the streets of Carthage carrying a picture of a creature who "had the ears of an ass, was hoofed in one foot, carried a book, and wore a toga." Accompanying the picture were the words: "The God of the Christians—born of an ass." It is clear from Tertullian, and other sources, that one of the rumors about Christians is that they worship a half-man, half-donkey.

This mockery of Christians also carried over to the stage. In the Roman theater, mime was a popular form of entertainment that included over-exaggerated characters, impossible storylines, and a special object of ridicule. We call such humor *farce*, a lower form of comedy of the likes of Monty Python or Mr. Bean. The object of ridicule was often a grotesque or deformed creature. It was this fool who was beaten for the amusement of the audience. What is more grotesque and deformed than an ass-man? On a bronze bowl from the first century AD there is depicted a man with a donkey's head being beaten by two other men in mimic dance. Could it be that the creator of the Alexamenos graffito had seen such a mime? Crucifixion was also a common subject in Roman mime. In the most popular mime of the first century AD, *Laureolus*, a runaway slave turned robber is crucified in the final scene. Historians record that so much artificial blood was used in the scene that during one performance the actor playing the slave fell over vomiting blood. The audience roared at the fate of the fool. How much more foolish then the ass-man of the *paedagogium*, the grotesque half-breed nailed to the cross like a rebellious slave? And what of Alexamenos? Was he not also a fool to regard this refuse of society as god and worship him as such?

In the summer of 202 AD, Septimius Severus issued an edict making it illegal to convert to Judaism or Christianity. This decree, released from the imperial palace just up the Palatine Hill from the *paedagogium*, sparked persecution against Christians across North Africa and Egypt. It was during this time that Tertullian wrote his *Apology* to refute the lies spread about Christians. Clement of Alexandria, a theologian and church father, was killed for his faith during this purge. Leonidas, the father of Origen, was also martyred. According to tradition, Origen, who, in his youthful exuberance, wanted to stand for his faith and die with his father, was saved only by the swift thinking of his mother who hid his clothing to keep him inside.

During this century and the next a new fool emerged as the star of the mime—the Christian. Perhaps it was this persecution that emboldened Alexamenos' colleague to mock him publicly. Or maybe the graffito was the result of simple youthful rivalry. We cannot know the direct cause. However, the purpose of the graffito is clear: to shame the follower of the crucified god. The cross as a symbol of shame is not surprising, nor should it have been to Alexamenos. Only a century and a half earlier, the apostle Paul wrote, "For consider your calling, brothers: not many of you were wise according to worldly standards, not many were powerful, not many were of noble birth. But God chose what is foolish in the world to shame the wise; God chose what is weak in the world to shame the strong; God chose what is low and despised in the world, even things that are not, to bring to nothing things that are."[1] As a Christian, Alexamenos would understand this. He would know that following Jesus meant walking through shame, for that is what his God did for him. As it is written in the letter to the Hebrews, "and let us run with endurance the race that is set before us, looking to Jesus, the founder and perfecter of our faith, who for the joy that was set before him endured the cross, despising the shame, and is seated at the right hand of the throne of God."[2] This was the Christian message. Jesus, the Son of God, became like an ass-man on the cross, so that slaves of men, like Alexamenos, could become sons of God.

What happened to Alexamenos? How did he respond to this mockery? We don't know. Did the persecution extend beyond graffiti on the walls? Did he continue to serve in the imperial court? Did he give in to the shame or remain true to his faith? These questions will remain an historical mystery. However, the walls of the *paedagogium* provide one final glimpse at the story. In an adjoining building of the same complex another significant etching was discovered on the walls. It reads, simply, *Alexamenos fidelis*. Alexamenos is faithful.

1. 1 Corinthians 1:26–28
2. Hebrews 12:1b–2

21.

Honor or Shame?

"He was despised and rejected by men, a man of sorrows and acquainted with grief; and as one from whom men hide their faces he was despised, and we esteemed him not."

—ISAIAH 53:3

A FEW DAYS BEFORE Christmas 2013, Justine was waiting in London's Heathrow Airport on her way to visit family in South Africa. Before boarding the plane, she tweeted to her 170 Twitter followers, "Going to Africa. Hope I don't get AIDS. Just kidding. I'm white!" When the plane began taxiing to the runway, she switched her phone to airplane mode and leaned back to sleep through the eleven-hour flight.

By the time Justine's plane landed in Cape Town, her life was upended. Three hours into the flight a popular blogger saw her message and retweeted it to his 15,000 followers. From there, Justine's words burned through the internet. The reaction was not positive. Threatening comments filled her twitter feed. Messages poured into her company's inbox demanding her dismissal. The hashtag #HasJustineLandedYet trended as everyone waited for her to turn on her phone and realize her life was ruined. There was too much irony for the internet to pass up (Justine was the global public relations director for a large media company), and so, the internet unleashed the shame.

When Justine finally reconnected to the internet in South Africa, she was in disbelief. There were messages from concerned friends, threats from strangers, a dismissal letter from her boss, and the realization that millions of people knew of her fate before she did. And she was not the only one affected. Justine's parents, whose passion was for racial reconciliation among white and black Africans, were angry and ashamed. Their work had been diminished and their political allies distanced. Justine had experienced the wrath of the internet and faced our modern equivalent of public shaming.

Public shaming is a phenomenon that stretches back through recorded history. Shame plays a constraining role in society, creating boundaries to prevent unaccepted behavior. In its simplest form, this shame is applied through words: "Shame on you" or "You should be ashamed of yourself." The loss of respect, or the general feeling of shame, is often enough to cause the individuals to rethink or change their actions. However, more forceful shaming has also been employed. Public discipline, like whippings or the stocks, were designed to not only inflict pain on the transgressor but to also bring on them the shame of the community. In this sense, the cross is the ultimate form of public shaming.

It is interesting that, when talking about a case like Justine's, we might say, "They crucified her for her tweet." We automatically recognize the connection between the cross and shame. This shame has two sides. When an individual was suspended on a pole or cross in the middle of the community, whether alive or dead, it was a public rejection of him and his family. His name became associated with someone outside the boundaries of acceptance. It was a shame from which he could never recover.

As if this was not enough, there was another aspect to the shame. There was an understanding in the community that the individual was not only rejected by man but also by the gods/God. How could the divine allow such shame to come upon someone they favored? This idea was also present for the Israelites. In the Law, Moses gives specific instructions concerning those hung on a tree. "And if a man has committed a crime punishable by death and he is put to death, and you hang him on a tree, his body shall not remain all night on the tree, but you shall bury him the same day, for a hanged man is cursed by God."[1] The presence of his body on the tree was proof that God had rejected him. This is the double blow of the cross—the shame of communal rejection and the shame of rejection by God.

Jesus told a story connected to this idea of shame. There was a man who had two sons. The older son was the obedient, respectable, accepted

---

1. Deuteronomy 21:22–23a

member of society. The younger was impatient, impulsive, and unwise. The story begins when the younger son asked his father for his share of the inheritance. In that time, much like today, to ask for your inheritance while your parents are still alive is akin to saying, "I wish you would hurry up and die, so I can get on with my life." Such a request would have brought shame upon the son and the father. The father called for the official inheritance documents and instead of writing his son out of the will as was expected, he honored his son's request and divided up his property. The foolish son quickly liquidated the property, cashed out his investments, and rushed off to explore the distant world. You can almost hear the gossip in the town. "Wow, he just couldn't wait to get rid of the old man!" "He took the money and ran!" The son not only brought shame upon himself but also on the whole family.

The young man spared no expense in his hedonistic journey. A flash of coin and he was surrounded by the pleasures of the world. However, his reckless living quickly exhausted his inheritance. The double blow of foolish behavior and economic downturn left him in need of basic necessities. The "friends" who had been quick to help him lighten his purse, now vanished into the crowd. He was forced to take a job working in the field with the pigs. For a Jewish boy, this was the bottom of the pit. Racked by hunger, he even longed to eat the pig food to survive.

It was at this point that the young man came to his senses. Remembering his father's house, he noted that even the servants lived better than he was living now. Perhaps his father would have it in his heart to allow him to work as a servant. At least then he wouldn't starve. With this thought in mind, he began the long journey back home.

Jesus' audience would have been hanging on His words. What will happen when the son reaches the village? How will the father respond? Will the father forgive his shameful son and allow him to serve in his house? There were certain elements the audience expected to happen. When a family member married an unfit woman, or sold family land to a foreigner, the community would gather together for a ceremony called *kezazah*. In the ceremony, a large jar was brought to the square and, in the presence of the shameful family member, the jar was broken. This action symbolized cutting off the person from the family. Through *kezazah* the family protected its honor and preserved its place in the community. This would have been in the minds of Jesus' audience.

As the son approached his village, he was apprehensive. The clothes he wore when he left his family were now unrecognizable. He was covered full body in pig filth. He brought with him no gifts for his family, as was the custom; he came empty-handed and in need. Despite the public shaming he expected from his community, he kept repeating the words in his head, "Father, I have sinned against heaven and before you. I am no longer worthy to be called your son. Treat me as one of your hired hands." Perhaps with time, he could earn enough money to buy back the land and redeem himself in the eyes of his family and community.

While the son was still a long way off, his father saw him. He was waiting for his son's return. Then, this elder of the community did a shocking thing: he lifted his cloak and ran toward the son. In Jesus' society, an older man would never run, much less hitch up his cloak and bare his legs. Elders moved slowly and deliberately in accordance with their age and station. Yet the father raced out to his son. When he reached him, the father embraced his lost son, his cloak pressing against the son's filthy skin, and kissed his matted head. The son launched into his prepared speech. "Father, I have sinned against heaven and before you. I am no longer worthy to be called your son." The father stopped him before he could finish and turned to his servant. "Bring the best robe and put it on my son. Put a ring on his hand and shoes on his feet. Kill the fattened calf. Let us eat and celebrate the return of my son. He was dead, and is alive again; he was lost, and is found."

Jesus, as a master storyteller, incorporated familiar scenarios into his stories. I am sure every village had at least one wayward son who brought shame onto his family. Maybe they had even witnessed a cutting off ceremony before. They never expected the father to shame himself in order to cover the shame of the son. Nor did they expect the father to honor the son with a celebration. Though the son deserved shame—the worst and most public shaming—his father gave him honor instead. In a way, the father shielded the son from shame by taking the shame upon himself. In love, the father replaced the son's shame with honor.

How does this story relate to the cross? The Bible makes clear that Jesus went to the cross willingly. Three times in Luke's gospel he predicted His death. In John, he stated, "I lay down my life that I may take it up again. No one takes it from me, but I lay it down of my own accord."[2] Why would anyone take up such a shameful end willingly? Why would anyone choose

2. John 10:17–18

to face the shame of both the community and God? For the same reason the father ran out to his son—out of love.

The author of Hebrews wrote that Jesus "for the joy that was set before him endured the cross, despising the shame . . ."[3] Jesus was not ignorant of the pain and shame associated with the cross. Yet despite that knowledge, he went willingly to his death. Like the father running out to his shameful son, Jesus ran to the cross out of love. Just as the father wrapped his arms around his son to protect him from the judgment of the community, so Jesus spread His arms on the cross to protect us from the shame we deserve. The only honorable one was put to shame so that we, who deserve shame, could receive honor.

If we are honest, we are much more like the shameful son than the disgraced Justine. We have done more than send a careless tweet. We regularly bring shame upon ourselves through our thoughts and actions. That is why we blush when we are caught in our jealousy, lies, or selfishness. That is why we hide our mistakes. Not only do we fall short of God's external standards, we cannot even live up to our internal ones. We are like the son standing at the edge of the town covered in the filth of our choices. We know we deserve what's coming to us.

Yet, we see Jesus running toward us. He has His robes in His arms and they are flapping around His bare legs. He is running to cover our shame. Paul described it this way, "Christ redeemed us from the curse of the law by becoming a curse for us—for it is written, 'Cursed is everyone who is hanged on a tree.'"[4] For those who place their faith in Christ alone, on the cross there was a trade: our shame and curse on Christ, His honor and blessing on us.

3. Hebrews 12:2
4. Galatians 3:13

22.

He Is Everything to Me

"I am trying here to prevent anyone saying the really foolish thing that people often say about Him: I'm ready to accept Jesus as a great moral teacher, but I don't accept his claim to be God. That is the one thing we must not say. A man who was merely a man and said the sort of things Jesus said would not be a great moral teacher. He would either be a lunatic—on the level with the man who says he is a poached egg—or else he would be the Devil of Hell. You must make your choice. Either this man was, and is, the Son of God, or else a madman or something worse. You can shut him up for a fool, you can spit at him and kill him as a demon or you can fall at his feet and call him Lord and God, but let us not come with any patronizing nonsense about his being a great human teacher. He has not left that open to us. He did not intend to."

—C.S. LEWIS, MERE CHRISTIANITY

I REMEMBER WHEN, A few years ago, the 33 foot cross was erected on Zlatište, a part of the mountain Trebević above Sarajevo. It was built overnight without the necessary permits or permission from the government. In the war, Zlatište was on the front lines, and just a couple of meters from the cross was a mortar and sniper den, whose remains can still be seen today. The president of the Association of Concentration Camp Survivors of Republika Srpska said in the media that the cross was erected as a memorial of remembrance for the Serbs that were killed in Sarajevo during the war, while in the print media the citizens of Sarajevo thought that a cross in that particular place was a memorial to killers, not victims. The Office of the High Representative (OHR—an international institution responsible for overseeing implementation of civilian aspects of the peace agreement ending the war in BiH) emphasized that religious symbols must not be used to intentionally incite ethnic tensions.

Just one day after the cross was set up, some young men from Sarajevo, one of whom was a juvenile, tried to knock down the newly-built cross and were arrested by the police in Serb Sarajevo. A few months later, two of them returned to Zlatište, waited for the Republika Srpska police who were guarding the cross to leave, and, a little after midnight, knocked it down.

Looking back at who I was before the war, when I was an atheist, I might have been one of those tearing down the cross. But at the moment, my feelings were mixed. I wasn't happy that some people incited ethnic tensions by erecting the symbol of my Savior's suffering, while on the other hand, I wasn't happy that some other people knocked down a symbol that has come to mean so much to me. I wasn't happy that the symbol of the cross was misused. Imagine me—the one who hated the cross, the one who made fun of those who believed in Jesus, the one who asked Sanja to stop going to church and to take off her cross earrings if she wanted to date— bothered by the denigration of the cross? That symbol, which I myself once hated, which I mocked, had become a holy symbol to me.

On the cross, Jesus died, and it wasn't an ordinary death but a hard, torturous death. He gave His life so that I could be free, and He died to take the punishment for my sin and for yours! Probably the most quoted verse in the Bible says, "For God so loved the world, that he gave his only Son, that whoever believes in him should not perish but have eternal life."[1] On the cross Jesus gave His life that I could have life, and not only eternal life in Paradise with Him, but that this life I live on the earth could have meaning and fulfillment. Jesus presents himself as a shepherd, the Good Shepherd who cares for His sheep, who came so the sheep could have life, life in abundance. He contrasts himself with the enemy, the devil, who came to steal, kill, and destroy.

Even when I hadn't yet accepted Jesus as my Lord and Savior, I knew well what sin was, what hate was, what turmoil was, what unforgiveness was, what jealousy was, etc. From the moment I repented of my sins and decided to follow Jesus, I started to learn what love, peace, and forgiveness are . . . and to find the full meaning of life. Not only that I now have eternal life, but God is changing me, so that I can enjoy this life more, and enjoy it

1. John 3:16

regardless of circumstances, worries, and problems that sometimes come along.

When they misdiagnosed my second tumor, the doctors gave me the wrong treatment and it damaged my right kidney. Before chemotherapy, my right kidney was 5 inches long, and after treatment it was only 3 inches. The doctors said it was still functioning a little, and I didn't need to do anything about it until it started to cause other health problems. I asked what kind of problems it could cause, and, among other things, they mentioned high blood pressure. In December 2015, I started to feel moderate pain in that right kidney, and after a visit to the urologist he sent me to do a scintigraphy. Before the scintigraphy, the nurse checked my blood pressure. As soon as she saw the numbers, she went and got the doctor—it was 210/130, and normal is 120/80. The kidney needed to be taken out.

After a few months of twists and turns with our health system, the operation was scheduled and performed on April 21, 2016. I went into the operating room with two kidneys and came out with one. They took me to intensive care to recuperate, but I felt really bad. I complained to the medical staff, and they assured me that it was a difficult operation and that I wouldn't feel tip-top for a while.

The next day, the head nurse noticed something strange coming out of the drain tube. Moments later I passed out. During the operation, they had nicked my intestines without noticing it. My stomach was in chaos. It took an emergency surgery, two surgeons, and an incision across my whole stomach, to save my life. After the second operation, I had a long recovery period, including a blood infection, a lung infection, and a blood clot in my lungs—instead of a few weeks of recovery it took six months. In spite of everything, I knew that I was a child of God, redeemed and justified by Jesus' sacrifice on the cross. In the Bible it is written that God works all things together for good for those who love Him. What good could come from the mistakes of these doctors? Why did God allow this?

This I know, even if I had died on the operating table, God would have worked it out for good. I know where I'm going after death. I'm going into an eternity with God. Two thousand years ago Jesus died on the cross, and on the third day He rose again. The Bible says He went to heaven to prepare a place for us, and that human eye has not seen nor has human ear heard all the good things God has prepared for us who are justified by Jesus' sacrifice. Because of this, I don't fear death, on the contrary, I anticipate it with a strange impatience. But I know that God is not finished with me on earth,

He still has work for me here and that brings me joy. When the time comes for me to move to that world, I don't even fear for my children if I go first.

As I'm writing this, Jovana is 21 years old and David is 17. Both of them have accepted Jesus as their Lord and Savior; they follow Him and serve Him. Jovana leads the youth group in church and is involved in some other church activities. David plays every Sunday on our worship team, leading us to worship God in music and song. I know that God loves them more than I could ever love them, He will take care of them like He has taken care of me and every one of His children. That's why I have no fear. Through the long physical recovery, He was working on me, building my character, developing my patience, and helping me see how some of my priorities were upside down.

When I had cancer the first time, I thought I had learned to set my priorities straight, but when it happened a second time, I was surprised how quickly I forgot what I had learned. Through the problems with my kidney I wasn't surprised anymore, but I saw how much I still have to learn. I came through every experience different; I came through more like Jesus. I am far from perfect, but I'm changing into His image and I'm trying to live a life pleasing to Him.

Today when I look back at my life, I see God's hand was always on me. From that day, so long ago, May 1969, when my mother Gordana got up early, hung the wash, and then went to the hospital with a big stomach, only to return a few days later, to the joy of my father and sister, with me and without the big stomach—from that very day, I see God's hand in my life. I see how life without Him has no meaning. Jesus is the one who sought me, and reached out to me, even when I rejected Him and ran from Him, while I cursed Him, and made fun of those who believed in Him, while I lied, cheated and stole—He waited patiently for me.

He used many things in my life to mold me and change me, to bring me to Himself and to show me His love. He showed me the greatest love on that awful cross—while He hung there, while blood ran down His face, while He received blows and insults, He thought of me. And He thought of you! That's why I get angry when people misuse the symbol of the death and suffering of my Savior for their own purposes, for purposes that too often are not only in conflict with God's will but totally against it.

That symbol, the cross, doesn't have any miracle-working power in and of itself, and nowhere in the Bible does it say we need to put it on a chain around our necks, or put it in our places of worship, or hang it on our walls, or set it on a hill above our towns. The first few centuries early Christians didn't even use it as a recognized symbol. I'm not saying it is wrong to use it or to wear it as jewelry. I'm not bothered anymore when Sanja puts on cross earrings. But it is only a symbol, a picture of the torture device on which Jesus received the death sentence. It was not a punishment for His sins, He was the only One without sin, but He paid the penalty for my sins, and for yours. That's why I love the cross, because it reminds me of God's unconditional love and grace shown to me on the cross, and that's why I get angry when people misuse it, abuse it, and belittle it.

23.

The Merciless Cross

"Can any man be found willing to be fastened to the accursed tree, long sickly, already deformed, swelling with ugly welts on shoulders and chest, and drawing the breath of life amid long-drawn-out agony? He would have many excuses for dying even before mounting the cross."

—SENECA

THE ROMANS DIDN'T INVENT crucifixion, that honor belongs to the empires of the east. The first recorded "execution by suspension" was in the 9th century BC under Shalmaneser, the king of Assyria. In this case, the victim was impaled on an upright post, feet clear of the ground, and displayed publicly. The Persians systematized this form of execution in the 5th century. It was Alexander the Great, though, who made the transition from impalement to crucifixion as we think of it today. In 332 BC, he had two thousand opponents hung on crosses along the Mediterranean coast outside the city of Tyre. A century later, during the Punic Wars, the Romans learned the practice and soon became its primary practitioners. Over the next five hundred years, they refined the bloody process to maximize its effects. According to Cicero, a Roman statesman and contemporary of Crassus, crucifixion was "the most shameful, painful and abhorrent of all executions." Roman citizens were usually spared from such a gruesome punishment. Crucifixion was primarily a punishment for slaves, although it was extended to violent criminals, military enemies and foreigners. Often it was used to suppress political dissent. Josephus reports that Titus crucified five hundred Jews a day outside the walls of Jerusalem during the siege of 70 AD in order to terrorize the citizens and force a surrender. The soldiers, making a sport of it, tried to come up with the most creative ways of nailing a man to a cross. Crucifixion was a message, written in the pain of the crucified and publicly proclaimed. This message the Romans perfected.

Consider the poor man condemned to crucifixion. His heart drops the moment he realizes his fate. Since crucifixion is a public affair, he has witnessed the agonizing event before. He knows what awaits him and the knowing is an agony in itself. The soldiers strip him and bind him to a column in the courtyard. According to Roman law, a person condemned to death was to first be scourged. He is bent over exposing his back, buttocks, and legs to the bite of the whip *(flagrum)*. As the leather tongs meet his back, he feels the lead balls (that are tied onto the ends of the cords) bruise his side and crack against his ribs. The shock awakens his senses, his heart quickens and blood rushes to the site of the blow. What he doesn't feel at first are the sharp pieces of sheep bone that are also tied into the leather strips. Then the soldier yanks back on the whip. An involuntary scream escapes his throat as the bone-shards take pieces of his flesh with them. The blood, coursing toward the site of the first blow, arrives just in time to spill down his back and onto the ground. In a flash of despair, he realizes the pain has only just begun. If he survives the scourge, which is not a guarantee since there is no limit of blows in Roman law, only more pain awaits. At that moment, the second soldier brings his flagrum down across his back. Again, the cracking of ribs and the ripping of flesh. This process repeats itself until he loses count. Slumping down against the binds on his wrist, he struggles to keep conscious as his life-blood wets the white stones around him. The blows continue to rock him with rhythmic destruction, but shock has set in, and it feels like he is watching the event from outside his body. His whole backside is a mush of bloody flesh. Each breath is labored, as broken ribs press into the soft flesh of his lungs. It is as if they are scourging his insides as well. At last, the centurion overseeing the crucifixion (exactor mortis) orders the soldiers, now breathless and flushed, to let down their whips. They release the man's bonds, and he crumples into a pool of his own blood. *Why did they stop?* He thinks. *Why couldn't they just kill me here?* He would take any fate other than what awaited him next.

The man hears the centurion give an order as rough hands pull him to his feet. Standing reawakens the feeling in his legs and back, and the sting of open wounds shoots through his body. He is surrounded by four soldiers. He knows they will not leave his side until the end. It is these men who will oversee his crucifixion, and it is their sadistic creativity that will determine his suffering. He winces as a seventy-pound beam is placed across his bloodied shoulders. The weight exacerbates the ache of his broken ribs. The blood loss is taking its toll on his body. In another time and place, carrying such a weight would have been easy. But this was not any beam, it was a *patibulum,* the horizontal beam of the cross. One of the soldiers jabs him in the back with the butt of his spear, reopening blood vessels and propelling him forward. He stumbles out of the courtyard and onto the main road heading out of the city. Citizens gather along the street to watch the procession. How many times had he been in their place—scoffing, spitting, mocking the poor stumbling fool? Now he is the fool, the *crucarius*. Before him walks a herald carrying the *titulus* on which is written the charges against him. Not only is he naked and beaten, stumbling through the streets of his hometown, but his guilt is proclaimed publicly. The shame is worse than the curses from the crowd. The walk is exhausting as the rough wood digs into his exposed flesh preventing capillaries from closing. He stumbles, falls, and the *patibulum* lands heavily on his back. What little air he had in his lungs is forced out. When he gets back to his feet, he finds it even more difficult to breath. His body screams for relief, but he knows none will come.

The procession exits the city gate and arrives at a small hill along the main road. The site was chosen for its prominent position. No one can enter or exit the city without seeing, hearing, and smelling the crucified man. Crucifixions were frequent enough that the vertical beam of the cross (*stipes*) remained in the ground year-round. The soldiers remove the beam from the man's shoulders. He enjoys a second of respite before hearing the clink of metal on metal. He sees four iron nails in one of the soldier's hands, each around six inches long and rusty from use. The nails are thick at the top, with large square heads, and taper down to a sharp point. The soldiers lay him down in the dust, the stray rocks embedding in his wounds, and stretch his arms out along the *patibulum*. The first soldier places the tip of the nail on his wrist, a thumbs width down from the palm. The man closes his eyes. With one blow the soldier drives the nail through his flesh and into the beam. The iron parts his carpal bones, injuring the median nerve and sending waves of lightning-bolt pain down his arm. The man's screams drown out the sound of the hammer on metal as the soldier drives the spike further into the wood. A second soldier repeats the process on his other wrist with the same agonizing effect. He had seen men remain defiant even from the cross, hurling curses on the Romans with their dying breath. But every man, no matter how strong, cried out when the nails went through the flesh.

The soldiers force the man to stand. He feels his feet leave the ground as the soldiers lift him and the *patibulum* to which he is attached. As the beam is inserted into the mortise of the *stipes*, the jolting movement sends flashing torment up his arms. He cries out. His legs are bent and pressed to the side of the upright beam. He hears the clink of metal seconds before feeling the torture of iron piercing his foot. With a flash of white he loses consciousness, only to awaken moments later as a nail goes through his other heel. The soldiers step back to admire their work. His feet are no more than a few feet off the ground. He is close enough to hear the conversations of passers-by on the road, to see the look on their faces when they behold him, to watch them look away in disgust. Satisfied, they find a spot to wait for the inevitable.

As the hours pass, the pain does not subside. Like a sore tooth, the nerves in his wrist become increasingly inflamed until even a light breeze on his skin is excruciating. During the night, a pack of dogs is drawn by the stench of blood. They circle the cross and snap at his feet. The soldiers, sitting around their fire, watch with excitement. The man tries to scare the pack away, but to no avail. The dogs eventually leave with the parts of his feet they can reach.

Slowly, his body begins to shut down. The hypovolemic shock from massive blood loss has taken a toll on his internal organs. His pulse quickens and his blood pressure drops—the heart's attempt to overcome the effects of hanging by his wrists. His breathing is labored. Each breath requires him to push up with his legs, rubbing his raw back against the splintered wood and ensuring fresh blood continues to flow. He feels life slipping away and yet, the torment continues. It is not until the second night that respiratory failure and the severe dilation of his capillaries results in multi-organ failure. At last, his suffering ends, although his shame does not. In the morning, the soldiers leave what is left of the man nailed to the cross. There he remains for three days until a relative claims his body. It is understandable why Josephus called crucifixion "the most cruel and atrocious of punishments."

Seneca, a Stoic philosopher and tutor to Emperor Nero, preferred suicide to the cross. "Can anyone be found who would prefer wasting away in pain dying limb by limb, or letting out his life drop by drop, rather than expiring once for all? Can any man be found willing to be fastened to the accursed tree, long sickly, already deformed, swelling with ugly welts on shoulders and chest, and drawing the breath of life amid long-drawn-out agony? He would have many excuses for dying even before mounting the cross." The cross was indeed excruciating (literally, in Latin, *ex-crux*, from the cross).

To what can the cross be compared? It has been said that wearing a cross pendant around your neck is like putting an electric chair or guillotine on a golden chain. But the reality of crucifixion destroys that comparison. The guillotine was created to provide a quick and painless death for the executed. Death by electrocution was performed in a private corner of a prison. Could there be a less relevant comparison to the public shame and suffering of the cross? It is difficult to find a modern parallel to the cross without looking to horror films or the work of deranged serial killers. Ivo Andrić came closest in his description of an impalement in his Nobel Prize winning work *The Bridge over the Drina*. The monstrosity of the cross highlights the power of the singular event that transformed it from a symbol of grotesque suffering to one of hope and victory.

On a Friday in 33 AD, the Romans, at the request of the religious leaders in Jerusalem, tried to send a message by crucifying Jesus of Nazareth on a hill outside the city. There should have been nothing spectacular about this cross on a hill—just one more poor fool crushed beneath the might of Rome—but the message backfired. On the third day after the crucifixion, news began to spread that Jesus' tomb was empty. Fifty days later, his followers, who should have been demoralized by the death of their leader, began preaching a message of repentance and proclaiming a baptism in the name of the crucified and risen Christ. Thousands responded to their call. The movement spread quickly despite persecution from the Jewish religious establishment and the Roman authorities. Followers of Jesus gave up their lives willingly, dying with His name on their lips. The Roman message failed and instead became a movement.

Jesus' death transformed the meaning of the cross. No longer was the cross simply an instrument of torture or a spectacle of shame, it was the stage on which Jesus Christ demonstrated His power and victory. The Roman cross had lost its power over Jesus' followers. Is it any wonder this movement has spread to the four corners of the earth?

Over the past two thousand years, many other meanings have been attached to the cross, whether through Constantine's sign or Pope Urban's speech or Scotland's traditions. These only serve to confuse the question.

Today's cross on a hill, be it Zlatište or Hum, should not be allowed to overshadow *the* cross on *the* hill two millennia ago. The true meaning of the cross is found in the one who faced the wrath of Rome and won. On the merciless cross the unmeasurable mercy of God was displayed.

24.

Suffering or Glory?

"Just as Christian came up to the Cross, his burden loosed from off his shoulders, fell from off his back, and began to tumble down the hill, and so it continued to do till it came to the mouth of the sepulchre. There it fell in, and I saw it no more!"

—JOHN BUNYAN

A FEW YEARS AGO, I stood on the sand of a Roman amphitheater whose remains can be visited today in a town called Solin next to Split, Croatia. It is thought to be built in the second century, and that it could hold 18,000 spectators. Solin is famous for the amphitheater, as well as for being the birthplace of the Roman emperor Diocletian, whose palace even today forms the framework for the old town in Split, and from which Split got its name (from the Latin word *palato*—"palace"). Along with the reforms he introduced in the Roman Empire, Diocletian remains famous for his persecution of Christians. Even though he was tolerant toward them at the beginning of his rule, his tolerance towards Christians dissipated little by little through his reign. First, he discharged all Christians from the Roman Army, then, in 303 AD, he issued the first of four edicts for the persecution of Christians.

Up until Constantine came to power, Christians were under severe persecution, including seizure of property and burning of their books and texts, and Christians themselves were imprisoned, tortured, and killed, often in the arena, where they died in gladiator battles or were torn apart by wild animals. The sands of the Solin Arena, on which I stood, were centuries earlier soaked with the blood of Christian martyrs. However, Diocletian didn't invent nor start the persecution of Christians.

One of the first records of the persecution of Jesus' followers is found in the book of Acts when Stephen was stoned to death, and then, shortly afterwards, the Pharisee Saul persecuted the followers of "the Way" and threw them into dungeons.[1] Unfortunately, even after Diocletian's death and Constantine's revocation of the edicts concerning the persecution of Christians, persecution didn't go away. Throughout history, we see, from the very beginning until today, many Christians suffered because of their faith in Christ.

In former Yugoslavia we were lucky to experience one of the milder forms of Communism where religion was tolerated to a point, but in some Communist countries Communism tried to completely eradicate Christianity, just like Diocletian attempted. Still today, I remember one of the first Christian books I read, *Tortured for Christ,* in which Romanian pastor, Richard Wurmbrand describes the torture he went through in Communism because of his faith. They beat him, brutally struck him, shocked him with electricity, burned his skin with cigarettes, left him wet in cold temperatures, etc. He felt the effects for the rest of his life.

Then I remember many friends who are rejected by family and friends because of their decision to follow Christ. When my wife, Sanja, decided to get baptized her parent's first reaction was that they didn't want to hear from her anymore. The father of a young man who I was going to baptize a few years ago threatened Josh and me with death, saying he would kill his son first and then us. In addition to suffering inflicted by other people, there is so much suffering, when I look at my life and those around me, from natural sources. I know Christians who are sick, unemployed, tired, exhausted, etc. I had cancer twice, I went through aggressive chemotherapy and during that time I lost sixty-five pounds, and all the hair and nails on my body. I had a kidney removed. If Christianity is good news, if Jesus won the victory on the cross, and if He defeated Satan, why do we suffer?

In the letter to the Philippians, the author encourages us to follow Jesus' example. In the second chapter, verses 5–11 it says, "Have this mind among yourselves, which is yours in Christ Jesus, who, though he was in the form of God, did not count equality with God a thing to be grasped, but emptied himself, by taking the form of a servant, being born in the likeness of men. And being found in human form, he humbled himself by

1. Acts 7–9

becoming obedient to the point of death, even death on a cross. Therefore, God has highly exalted him and bestowed on him the name that is above every name, so that at the name of Jesus every knee should bow, in heaven and on earth and under the earth, and every tongue confess that Jesus Christ is Lord, to the glory of God the Father." So much is said in these few verses. We see that Jesus temporarily renounced His divine attributes and came into this world in human form because of His love for us. He was in all things like us, except for sin, humbling Himself to die on a cross.

As we saw earlier in this book and as we see in the Bible and in history, death on a cross is a horrible death, a death full of pain, suffering, and agony, but Christ, however, came through it all as a victor. These verses tell us that it was because Jesus chose suffering, because He chose that hard road, because of this, that He was again exalted to the highest place—that's why He won. In the book, *When Darkness Seems My Closest Friend,* my good friend Mark Meynell writes that the cross is the place where creation killed the Creator, the logical end of a road started when humans rejected God's authority in the beginning. This means, he says, that Christ's cross is the worst thing to happen in the history of humankind.

Furthermore, he writes, "Yet, the sight that comes from faith—in other words, the perspective shaped by what God has revealed and achieved—sees things very differently. It looks beyond appearances to the substance. To the eyes of faith, the cross is a victory and act of genius—the only place in human history where perfect justice has met with perfect mercy. So, what was the greatest event ever to take place on earth? The cross!" In the eyes of faith, the cross is not a defeat, but a victory. When we don't know the whole story, some battles can look to us like defeat, but when we know the end of the story, we see that it was really in those battles that the victory was won. When we think about Irenaeus, the leader of the church in Sirmium (now Sremska Mitrovica, Serbia) who was killed by the sword and thrown in the Sava River in 304 AD during Diocletian's reign, or Domnius, who started the church in Solin and was beheaded, most likely, in the same amphitheater where I stood a few years ago, we can't help think they were losers, because, in the end, they lost their lives due to their faith.

But let's look at what Jesus says, "Whoever finds his life will lose it, and whoever loses his life for my sake will find it." How can we make sense of these words? The Bible often tells us illogical or incomprehensible things, at first glance: the first will be last, and the last first, who is the greatest will be the servant of all, who dies will live. These things, called the upside down logic of God's Kingdom, will make complete sense one day when God's Kingdom comes in its fullness. One day, when we see the eternal reward that Irenaeus, Domnius, and all those who willingly suffered for Christ, received, it will be clear to us that they are not defeated, but victorious. We, Christians, believe in God but also in the enemy of God, the devil, who is real and who hates God and the object of God's love—God's creation. Much suffering comes from the devil and his hatred, from those who are not on God's side, from those who oppose God's work and His plan.

But not all suffering comes from this side. Sometimes we suffer because of our wrong choices; sometimes suffering is the consequence of our decisions. I met Nijaz a few years ago, and last year Nijaz died. Because he accepted Jesus as his Lord and Savior before his death I know that today he is in a better place, in heaven, a place without pain and suffering. But throughout his life, Nijaz suffered, especially in the last months when he was afflicted by the lung cancer that killed him. Nijaz was an avid smoker. Long ago, doctors started telling him to stop smoking, and, long ago, tobacco companies started putting warnings on cigarette boxes saying, "Smoking kills," but Nijaz ignored all the warnings, and, in the end, he bore the consequences of his decision. Because of his longtime addiction and his decision to continue smoking, he suffered.

Sometimes we suffer because of our decisions, and sometimes others suffer because of ours, and sometimes these decision are not just choosing to act, but also choosing not to act. In February 2008, a boy who went to the same school as my children entered a tram. Three stops later he lay dead on the floor of the tram, stabbed by three young bullies for looking at them. The tram was full of people, and no one reacted; no one did anything to protect Denis when the confrontation started. He was killed and his mother suffers today because of the decision of three minors to do something, and the decision of all the other people in the tram to do nothing.

God trusted us to govern this world, and we are responsible for it. Our decisions and choices must be good and correct, otherwise we ourselves, or someone else, will suffer. Sometimes we can't influence decisions because they are made by people in authority over our lives, and we can't reach them. When Diocletian decided to issue the edict to persecute Christians, the Christians in the Roman Empire could do little about it. When the politicians in former Yugoslavia decided to start a war in the 1990's, I couldn't do anything about it. But just as the Christian martyrs came through like victors after the persecution in the Roman Empire, so I came through the war a victor. Even though I lost my job, was without savings, had to leave my hometown and country . . . through wartime I found the greatest treasure I have today—a renewed relationship with my Creator and my Savior.

Sometimes God allows suffering so we can learn something, so our character can be changed, or simply so God can protect us. If we look at the world around us, at sports victories, war victories, musical successes, sufficient effort and "suffering" always stand behind them. My daughter trained in rhythmic gymnastics for many years, and now she is a trainer for the younger generation. When we watch these young girls gracefully execute all the complicated movements with smiles on their faces, taking home medals, we often forget the hours of effort and sweat, with the accompanying physical pain, that was necessary in training. My son is a musician. I remember many blisters on the tips of his fingers from practicing new chords. Jovana and David suffered to be formed, to learn new things, which brought them pleasure, happiness, joy, and praise in the future.

Today David uses his musical talent and performs in many concerts and every Sunday, he plays in church. He loves music. But I remember a time when he wanted to give up. If he had given up, he would have never found the happiness and pleasure that playing brings him. Sometimes we must go through tough times and problems to learn new things and to change. I'm not talking only about gaining intellectual knowledge or motor skills.

One of the hardest periods of my life was when I was diagnosed with cancer the first time. Even today I remember the time well, and I remember how I matured more in the few days after my diagnosis than a few years of "normal" life. Through that time I realized how out of order my priorities were and how I gave an important place to unimportant things in my life causing the important things to suffer. Today I thank God for that experience of suffering because I see how God used it to work on me and my character and change me for the better.

When I think about God allowing suffering in our lives to protect us, I remember when Jovana was a baby. In our apartment we had a large stove that would heat up so much at night that the metal door would glow red. Jovana was born in the summer and the first winter she spent in a crib. When she started crawling and walking the next summer, one of her favorite places to play was around the little door of the stove. She would open the door, set up her toys and then take them out. Sanja and I thought it was so cute, and we didn't think at all about what would happen when winter arrived. You can't explain to a child who's a year and some months old that she can't play with the stove door now because it is hot.

I knew we couldn't supervise her all the time, and that the moment would come when we would be distracted, and I was afraid that at that moment the skin of her palm would stick to the hot door. Then I thought of a solution. I heated the stove just enough to be hot to the touch, but not to burn, trying it first with my hand, then I sat in the armchair, took a newspaper and let Jovana play. After some time, she came to the stove and reached for the door. She screamed, started to cry, and looked at me with astonishment in her eyes. In that look, I could see her confusion: Why did her father who loved her, who was there next to her and could have stopped the pain and suffering, not do anything to stop it? In that moment, she couldn't understand I did it to protect her, she didn't know I tried my hand first to be sure she could safely pass through that experience of pain and suffering. But she did learn the lesson, and she never reached for that little hot door again.

The goal of this chapter is not to list all the reasons and possible causes of suffering in the lives of Christians. The goal is to introduce you to the fact that even when we become Christians and followers of Jesus, suffering won't necessarily discontinue and disappear. God is not a "wishing well" that answers every prayer by giving us what we want. Sometimes suffering is a direct result of our faith and decision to follow Christ, i.e., persecution, rejection from people, mocking. Still today people are killed for their faith in Christ. In the book of Philippians, Paul boasts about all the things people take pride in today—background, education, character, etc.—and then he says, "I count everything as loss because of the surpassing worth of knowing Christ Jesus my Lord. For his sake I have suffered the loss of all things and count them as rubbish, in order that I may gain Christ, . . . that I may know him and the power of his resurrection, and may share his sufferings, . . . I press on toward the goal for the prize of the upward call of God in Christ Jesus."[2]

If we doubt God can turn suffering into good, we need only to look to the cross where God turned the worst possible suffering into the greatest joy that we can imagine. I will conclude with the words of a man who knew about suffering, a man who was in dungeons, who was beaten, who was in mortal danger, who was whipped three times, stoned once, shipwrecked

2. Philippians 3:4–14

three times, who knew hunger and thirst, cold and nakedness.[3] He wrote, "For I consider that the sufferings of this present time are not worth comparing with the glory that is to be revealed to us."[4]

3. 2 Corinthians 11:23–33
4. Romans 8:18

25.

Retrospect

"I appeal to you therefore, brothers, by the mercies of God, to present your
bodies as a living sacrifice, holy and acceptable to God, which is your spiritual
worship. Do not be conformed to this world, but be transformed by the renewal
of your mind, that by testing you may discern what is the will of God, what is
good and acceptable and perfect."

—ROMANS 12:1–2

As I WRITE THIS I'm sitting in a hotel room in Poland where I am one of
the speakers at a large European conference with over seven hundred leaders from Europe and beyond. Yesterday was my 48th birthday. I spent the
whole day on the road, in a van with friends from Sarajevo. Twelve hours
of driving is not the ideal way to celebrate one's birthday. It caused me to
reflect on past years and past birthdays.

Twenty-five years ago, today, Sanja and Oleg sent me off on a plane
to Cyprus. Thirty years ago, I celebrated my "big" 18th birthday, the day
one comes of age. I remember that my mom was inviting relatives over
to the house to celebrate, but gave me money to take my friends out first.
She asked that I not stay out too late because family was coming to see me.
I went out with my friends to a restaurant called Labirint next to the Old
Bridge and drank a lot of alcohol. I arrived late, but when I got home my
cousins were still there. In the middle of the table was a tray of lamb that my
mom had prepared for dinner. I received congratulations, sat at the table,
and started to talk to the guests, but the smell of the food and the alcohol in
my body had their way. I vomited all over the table.

I went to my room, and lay on my bed, unable to close my eyes because the whole room would spin around me. My brother-in-law came in, pushed some money under my pillow, kissed me, and told me I was a grown man now. Not only was I not ashamed, but I was proud of my drunken state. Today I see how my values were out-of-order. When I worked in the casino, I stole, lied, got drunk, swore, and cheated and thought it was completely alright and that those things made me a real man. A transformation, that only God could do, needed to start in my life in order for me to realize life's true values and virtues. This transformation is still taking place and I'm still changing. The road ahead is long, but when I look back I see a long road behind me.

When the war started, we didn't have the means of communication that we have today. There were no mobile phones, text messages, internet connections, social networks, etc. When I left Mostar, I lost contact with almost all my friends and acquaintances. Years passed before I connected with some of them again. A few years ago, I traveled from Sarajevo to Mostar to teach the students in the Bible School. I used the afternoon to walk around and to drink coffee. To my great surprise, the waiter in the restaurant was my former colleague from the casino. We hadn't seen each other for twenty years, and I didn't know where he was or what had happened to him. He told me where he was living and invited me over.

When I visited him and his wife, he shared his story with me, and I found out he also left the city and went abroad at the beginning of the war. There he connected with an organization that controlled gambling in that town and continued to do the same work he did in Mostar. In the end, he was accused of murder, arrested, and sentenced to a long prison sentence. He was full of bitterness, claiming he had been falsely accused and unjustly convicted. Then I shared my life story with him. He told me that it was evident I had changed. He saw joy, peace, and hope in me. I knew that it was God who brought those things into my life, and I realized how thankful I should be for the transformation He began in me. If I didn't pray that first prayer in Mostar, and if, afterwards, I didn't "open" myself to God and His work, I could have easily ended up like my colleague in some jail full of bitterness and unforgiveness, or even worse like my former boss Žorž riddled with bullets in some underground garage.

Some changes were instantaneous. For example, swear words used to be my bywords, every other word out of my mouth, but a few days after I decided to accept Jesus as my Lord and Savior, I realized my vocabulary had changed. The swear words had been deleted. I didn't even try; it simply happened. Some other things needed more time. I was a heavy smoker for many years, having started in elementary school, and smoked, on average, two packs a day. I knew smoking wasn't good for my health, my wallet, or the environment and that it was an addiction I needed to resolve. I tried and tried to stop smoking, but I wasn't successful. I would quit smoking, but the longing for cigarettes wouldn't leave me. I wouldn't smoke for a few days or weeks, and then I would "fall" and start again. It was an endless cycle.

I prayed and asked others to pray for me, but there weren't any results until one evening nineteen years ago at a summer camp organized by our church. After the evening program, I stood on the terrace with a friend, and we talked. I shared with him my frustration with smoking, and he offered to pray for me. By then I had given up trying in my own strength and power, and had already prayed multiple times, "God, I can't change this in my strength and power, but I believe You, in Your grace, can take this addiction from me."

That night my friend prayed a short prayer for me, and I felt that something was different. I knew that God had somehow set me free from my addiction to nicotine. I went to my tent and told Sanja I wasn't a smoker anymore. She didn't believe me and said time would reveal the truth. Nineteen years have passed since then and not only do I not smoke, but I have never had a desire to light up a cigarette. I believe time did reveal. However, I don't think this means that God needs more time to change some things in our lives than others.

I have a friend, a pastor, who was a heroin addict before he decided to follow Jesus. One evening he prayed that God would free him from the heroin addiction, and when he woke up in the morning he felt strange. He wasn't immediately aware of what had happened but after some time realized that this was the first morning in a long time he didn't have a desire for drugs, and he wasn't thinking about heroin and how to get it. The freedom was instantaneous. While some people go through rehabilitation and other programs for years to break their addictions, God released him overnight. He wasn't a junkie anymore, and today he leads one of our churches and helps others find freedom from addictions.

A relationship with God changes us and transforms us. We become different, better, and our life priorities and goals change. This is a process that lasts our whole lives. God accepts us like we are with all our flaws, but

He wants us to change, to change us into His image. Besides prayer, which plays a key role in our life and our spiritual development, reading the Bible is also very important. We Christians believe that the people who wrote the Bible were inspired by God, and that the Bible is God's instructions for our lives. Most books we read are written to impart information, but the Bible, besides imparting information, has the potential to transform our lives. The condition is that we accept Jesus and desire to change into His image.

Prayer, reading the Bible, fellowship with believers, and other spiritual disciplines are not the means by which we achieve things or earn favor with God. In the Bible, it says that we are saved by grace through faith and that salvation doesn't come through us, it's a gift of God.[1] We can't and we don't need to add anything or take anything away from that which Jesus completed for us on the cross. However, our spiritual disciplines are a product of our faith and love for God, not a prerequisite.

For some time after I became a Christian and after I returned to Mostar, I didn't tell many people about my former life. Then one summer our church began some evangelistic activities on the street. In the late afternoon, we would play and sing some Christian songs at a place in town where people were out walking. Afterward, one of us would share how God changed his life. In the beginning, I stood on the side, scared a friend or acquaintance would see me and get a bad impression of me. Then I remembered my life before I met Jesus: I remembered my eighteenth birthday and how I shamed my mother, I remembered how I stole in the casino and how I stuck a pistol in a man's ribs and threatened him, I remembered how I once drove so drunk I fell asleep at a traffic light and my friend couldn't wake me up. I remembered that in those situations I wasn't ashamed—I was even proud of my sins, and bragged about it. I realized that I was on the right path and didn't need to be ashamed, but proud—proud of God and the change He was bringing in my life, proud of the work He was completing, proud of the eternal future I would spend with God because of what Jesus did for me on the cross. Then God put the desire in my heart to begin sharing the Good News, the news that God loves us, and provided a solution for our sins.

Today whenever I can, I use the opportunity to tell people about God's righteousness, love, and grace. Young people are especially interested in the part of my life when I was involved in organized crime, and how God changed me. I often speak to university students, speaking at more than 30

1. Ephesians 2:8

universities all over Europe in the past ten years. It's always a message about the sin that separates us from God, and a message about the love and grace of God. It is the message about Jesus, who died on a cross to pay the penalty for our sins with his life. It is the message that all who accept Jesus' work on the cross, who repent and decide to follow Him, are forgiven of their sins and can have a renewed relationship with their Creator, with God. It is the message about the cross of Jesus, the only place where God's righteousness and God's grace meet.

Conclusion

"I am the way, and the truth, and the life.

No one comes to the Father except through me."

—JESUS

IT WASHES WHITER, IT wastes less, it drives longer, it's the best, the cheapest, 100 free minutes, healthier, more natural, wrinkles disappear, muscles strengthened . . . We all are used to advertisements promising a product that is just the help we need. It doesn't take long before we determine their claims are not entirely true. It is like election campaigns and political parties. Vote for us, and if we win there will be more jobs, greater pensions, less taxes, new roads—you dream it, we will do it. Then when they come to power, they all too often forget their campaign promises. We in Bosnia and Herzegovina have a name for those kinds of advertisements and campaign promises that don't hold water. We call them hollow stories or empty promises. We are used to hollow stories and empty promises, we come across them in every segment of our lives.

Two years ago, when my blood pressure was quite elevated, the doctor prescribed an aggressive treatment to lower my pressure and told me that after my kidney was removed the treatment would no longer be necessary. After the operation, I realized these were empty words.

Can anyone be trusted today? People, hardly. But God is not like man, God is different. His stories hold water, they are not hollow, and His promises are not empty. On the contrary, God offers us empty evidence of a fulfilled promise.

What am I saying? The Gospels speak a lot about the day Jesus was crucified and about His death on the cross. In all four of the Gospels, we can read about that Friday evening when Joseph of Arimathea, one of Jesus' followers, came to Pilate and asked for Jesus' body so he could bury Him. After Pilate confirmed the information about Jesus' death with the centurion, he ordered Jesus' body removed from the cross, and given to Joseph so he could lay Him in a grave.[1] Jesus' dead body was removed from the cross, leaving the cross empty. What does the empty cross communicate? What kind of message does it send?

The empty cross speaks to us about the forgiveness of sin, or better said the redemption from sin, because our sins are not just forgiven, they are paid for. Jesus redeemed us with His life, the price was great. One of Jesus' last words on the cross was *tetelestei*, which in Greek means, "It is finished," or "it's over." In Jesus' time, this word was often used in the marketplace; when there was an outstanding debt and the debt was paid, they used the word *tetelestei*, meaning, it was finished, paid in full, the debt no longer existed. The empty cross reminds us of God's fulfilled promise regarding the forgiveness of sin.

Even in the Old Testament, God through the prophet Jeremiah spoke of a time when our sins would be no longer mentioned.[2] That time has come, that prophecy was fulfilled on the cross. Jesus died, the cross is empty, and everyone who puts their faith and trust in Jesus is forgiven of their sins. *Tetelestei*—it is finished!

As we read further through the Gospels, we see that on Friday evening Joseph wrapped Jesus in cloth, as was the custom at that time, and laid Him in a grave. The grave was sealed with a large stone, and Roman guards were stationed in front of the grave to keep watch. Saturday came and went. Sunday morning two Marys and Salome bought oil and went to the grave to anoint the dead body, as custom dictated at that time. On the way, they wondered who would roll the large stone from the entrance because they couldn't do it alone. But when they arrived, they found the stone already rolled away, and the tomb empty. Jesus had risen from the dead just as He had said.[3]

What does the empty tomb tell us? Of what does Jesus' empty tomb remind us? Jesus' empty tomb reminds us of God's fulfilled promise of the resurrection of the dead and of eternal life with God. The Bible says that our corruptible body will put on an incorruptible one, our mortal body will become immortality. The Bible and the empty tomb remind us that

1. Mark 15:42–47
2. Jeremiah 31:34
3. Mark 16:1–8

Jesus Christ gave us the victory over sin and over death, that in Him we have eternal life, and that the promise of resurrection from the dead will be fulfilled.[4]

Further in the Gospels we read that through the next couple of weeks, all the way to the ascension, Jesus met with His disciples, ate with them, talked with them, and taught them. The empty tomb reminds us that Jesus is alive today, and that we can have fellowship with Him through the Holy Spirit who came upon the believers at Pentecost as Jesus promised.[5] The empty tomb reminds us of the fulfillment of God's promise given through the prophet Zechariah, where He said we would be His people, and He would be our God, so we could have a relationship with Him. That promise is fulfilled in Jesus for everyone who accepts Him and repents of their sins.

The empty cross and the empty tomb are reminders for us of God's fulfilled promises.

In this book we tried to explain and to bring the reader closer to the true meaning of the cross. Jesus transformed both of our lives, and today they have purpose and meaning. We have experienced the forgiveness of sin, a renewed relationship with God, grace, peace, and joy.

And you? What do you think about this symbol, those two pieces of wood put together, and what Jesus completed on the cross? What do you think about all this after reading these pages? Are you ready to repent of your sins and accept Jesus? If you are, all you have to do is to pray the prayer which I prayed in Mostar, in the darkness of my room. Word order is not important, what's important is that with your mind and heart you believe what you are praying. You need to confess your sins to God, to thank Jesus that He was willing to give his life and pay the high price for your sins, and to ask him to take control of your life and accept Him as your Lord and Savior. I'm sure your life will never be the same. Making a covenant with God and putting everything into His hands is the best decision I ever made. You won't regret it either.

One last thing, you need to find a community of believers, a church, a group of people who try to follow Jesus and the teaching of the Bible. God created us for community. Jesus saved me, He changed my life, and in the church, with the help of older believers, I continue to grow. Don't hesitate, find a church where the emphasis is on the Bible and biblical teaching,

---

4. 1 Corinthians 15:54–57

5. Acts 1–2

where the truth of the Gospel is preached, and become a part. The blessings will be many.

If you have accepted Jesus and given Him your life, our prayer for you is the following:

> "The LORD bless you and keep you;
> the LORD make his face to shine upon you and be gracious to you;
> the LORD lift up his countenance upon you and give you peace."[6]

If you haven't made this decision to repent of your sins and accept Jesus, our prayer for you is that you don't postpone this decision but make it as soon as possible. No one knows how many days they have left in this life, nor when Jesus will come for His people, His church. Don't wait until it's too late!

6. Numbers 6:24–26

CPSIA information can be obtained
at www.ICGtesting.com
Printed in the USA
FFHW010143291218
50006084-54743FF